KANGAROO   FLYING STORK   WALKING STORK
CICADA   HORSE AND RIDER   COW
PALM TREE   DUCK   LIFE BOAT   CHINESE JUNK

PAPER TOY MAKING

BY

MARGARET W. CAMPBELL

FOREWORD
BY
R. R. TOMLINSON, R.B.A., A.R.C.A.

DOVER PUBLICATIONS, INC., NEW YORK

Published in Canada by General Publishing Company, Ltd., 30 Lesmill Road, Don Mills, Toronto, Ontario.

Published in the United Kingdom by Constable and Company, Ltd.

This Dover edition, first published in 1975, is an unabridged republication of the work originally published in 1937. The frontispiece and plates facing pp. 6, 40, and 56 were in full color in the original and are here reproduced in black and white. This Dover edition is published by special arrangement with the original publisher, Sir Isaac Pitman and Sons, Ltd., 39 Parker Street, London WC2B 5PB, England.

International Standard Book Number: 0-486-21662-4
Library of Congress Catalog Card Number: 75-2570

Manufactured in the United States of America
Dover Publications, Inc.
180 Varick Street
New York, N.Y. 10014

FOREWORD

"To those who, standing apart from the rush and flurry of life, look upon the world with a seeing eye, it is, surely, interesting to observe on what small and apparently insignificant things great matters depend. To the student, history abounds with examples, and to the philosopher they are to be met with everywhere."

Jeffery Farnol used these words for the opening of a chapter in *The Amateur Gentleman*; he might equally well have written them as an introduction to Mrs. Campbell's book.

Although this book presents something entirely new, it recognizes the urge of an instinct which is as old as life itself—the play instinct. The educationist is fully aware of the importance of stimulating a child's interest in its formative years. There is no better means of arousing his interest than by appealing to the play instinct, and at no time is his interest so completely absorbed as when he is playing with toys.

What small and apparently insignificant things are toys often thought to be; yet seldom is it realized how frequently the making of a toy decides the future career of a child.

Mrs. Campbell's book, *Paper Toy Making*, has the widest possible appeal, for the material advocated is within the reach of both rich and poor and the models it describes are equally attractive to both boys and girls.

Paper Toy Making has great possibilities for good for it has a place in the school as well as in the home.

As a pleasant and effective introduction to geometry it has no rival, and as a means of training the craftsman's fingers and the artist's colour and pattern sense, few activities could be more helpful, for coloured materials may be used, as the illustrations of the book show, and the models it contains lend themselves admirably for decoration.

Only too few of the activities of school life to-day can be carried on with equal facility and enjoyment in both the home and the school. It is of the utmost importance, however, that a child's leisure should be occupied to his physical and mental advantage.

It is because I firmly believe that every effort should be made to make the life of children as interesting and contented as possible, that I welcome the opportunity this foreword offers to express my convictions, as well as to wish the book success.

Mrs. Campbell has contributed in no small measure to the teachers' and the parents' equipment for the development of the child. She has enabled them to take a step forward towards making education a more natural and therefore more enjoyable form of development.

R. R. TOMLINSON

CHISWICK, 1936

v

TO MY

GRANDCHILDREN

PREFACE

My mother, the authoress and designer of this book, is now a grandmother of many children, to whom she is as great a luxury and delight as she was to her own large family.

She is the inventor of a child's *Euclid* in which the theorems are sheer amusements. But while amusing, this book cannot fail to inculcate the principles of architecture and design in children's minds.

Though she includes many of the traditional tricks, a great many more of these paper structures are of her own invention.

The Japanese, who are perhaps the world's ablest handicraftsmen, train their children on such amusements as these. With this book any child will have a private toy-factory at his disposal.

Our hands, the most beautiful and precise instruments that were ever created, are apt to be neglected. This is a button-pressing age in which the thumb rivals its more sensitive neighbours, but the surgeon, the architect, the artist and all other skilled workers, in fact all those who get the most pride and pleasure from their work, still rely on their hands.

There is no doubt that there is a real need for a book like this; and I have no doubt that it will have a grown-up public not only among invalids and others upon whose hands time hangs heavily, but among happy parents and all people who enjoy playing with children.

My first sensation of having created anything was when the flying bird (to be found in this book) first flapped its wings in my hands; and I shall not forget the miniature miracle of boiling water in a paper kettle over the flame of a candle. This hobby is full of homely wisdom. But it has also among its fanciers several very outstanding intellects: for example, Leonardo, Shelley, and Unamuno. I can quite imagine that the traditional flying bird might have been one of the lighter butterfly-fancies of Leonardo's brain when he was suddenly struck with the beauty or intelligence of a child, and turned aside to amuse him.

Shelley's paper argosies were the pastime of his youth and early manhood.

Unamuno, the greatest living Spaniard, is also a devoted grandparent, and one of his chief joys in his old age is folding paper toys for his little grandson.

With all respect to him—I have seen a trayful of his toys, but they are not to be compared with my mother's.

I wish all students of this book as much fun as my brothers and I got out of this paper magic, and as much fun as our children are getting.

ROY CAMPBELL

PLATES

CONTENTS

CONTENTS

PAPER TOY MAKING

INTRODUCTION

I HAVE taken a life-long interest in paper-folding, and when I reached the allotted span of life my family persuaded me to write a book on the subject. This book was written for my grandchildren only, without any idea of ever publishing it, so that explains the familiar wording throughout. One day Dr. Bews of Natal University College saw it, and said it was highly educational, and must be published.

I have found it quite impossible to describe in words many of the paper manipulations, and have resorted to diagrams, to help where words have failed; but if the directions are carefully followed and every stage is checked by the diagrams, even a beginner should be successful.

I learned much of my paper-folding in Japan, China, and other Eastern countries, where the children begin paper-folding from their babyhood. It is excellent manual training and cannot be begun too early. For that reason, I have begun my book with the most elementary folding, and if young children do these first it will help them greatly when they come to more intricate folding later on.

This pastime has been invaluable in whiling away the tedious hours for convalescent children, and amusing children of all ages.

I would advise beginners to use paper 6 in. square and to press the folds well. First press a fold with the forefinger, and then come back over it with the thumb-nail, to give each fold a clean sharp edge. This is very important. Folds are often made for the sake of the creases, which are left when the paper is unfolded. In some cases these creases act as guide-lines, but in others they function in making inverted pleats, which, if the creases are firmly made, fall into place with fascinating facility.

The best way to make the diagonal fold is to place the corner C exactly on A as shown in the diagram on page 2. Then hold the two points in position, by placing the left forefinger on the two corners A and C.

Then, with the right forefinger, follow the centre line from A to E; then press from E to D and then again from E to B.

Now, with your right thumb-nail, press heavily from B to D to get a clean sharp edge to your fold. Undo this, and lay flat; then fold the other diagonal line by raising B to D, and repeat the same process.

Gummed paper must be avoided. Squares of coloured paper may be bought in packets of 100. The thinnest toughest paper is best.

HILTON ROAD,
   NATAL,
     S. AFRICA.

                                   M. W. CAMPBELL

INTRODUCTION: MAKING THE DIAGONAL FOLD

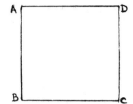 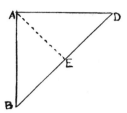

ENVELOPE

1. Fold a square of paper straight across in half; undo.
2. Fold across in half the other way; undo; lay flat and you have Fig. 1.
3. Now fold diagonally from corner to corner, placing *G* on *E*. Crease well along the centre line *FH*; undo.
4. Fold diagonally the other way, placing *F* on *H*; crease heavily along *EG*; undo and you have Fig. 2.
5. Fold *F* to the dot next to *O*.
6. Fold *H* to the dot next to *M*.
7. Fold *G* up to the dot next to *L*, on the line *EG*.
8. Fold point *E* down to the dot next to *N*.

Fig. 3 shows the envelope complete.

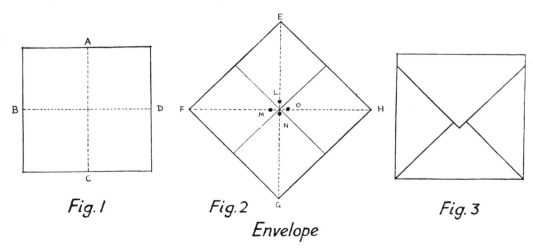

Fig. 1   Fig. 2   Fig. 3

Envelope

PICTURE FRAME

This requires a 6 in. square of paper.

1. Fold a square of paper diagonally both ways; undo.
2. Turn paper over and fold straight across both ways; undo.
3. Turn paper again, and lay flat.
4. Fold each corner to the centre, and you have Fig. 4.
5. Fold *E* to *A*, and *F* to *B*.
6. Fold *G* to *C*, and *H* to *D*, then you have Fig. 5.

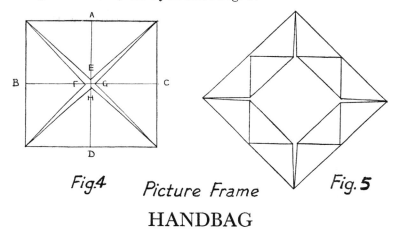

Fig.4   Picture Frame   Fig. 5

HANDBAG

This requires a 6 in. square of paper.

1. Fold a square of paper diagonally both ways; undo.
2. Fold the corners to the centre *E*, and you have Fig. 6.

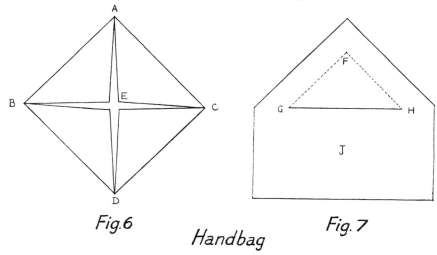

Fig.6   Handbag   Fig. 7

3. Fold *B* and *C* to *E*, then fold *D* to *A*, and you have Fig. 7.
4. Cut along dotted lines through all the layers with a sharp penknife.
5. Fold point *F* single layer only to *J*.
6. Turn figure over and repeat.
7. Cut away the inside parts that show between *F*, *G*, and *H*.

DRINKING-CUP

1. Fold a square of paper diagonally once, and you have Fig. 8.
2. Fold *F* to *B* along dotted line, so that *GF* is parallel to the line *DE*.
3. Fold *C* to the point *G* along dotted line, making the line *BC* fall on *FG*. Then you have Fig. 9.
4. Fold down the flap *A*, single layer only, as far as it will go in front.
5. Turn figure over and fold flap down on the other side. Then you have Fig. 10.

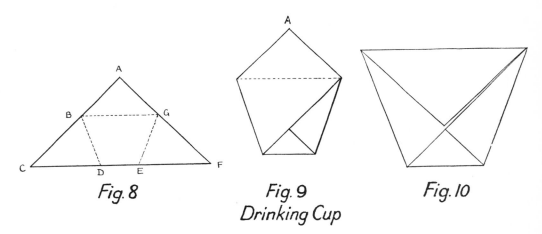

Fig. 8   Fig. 9   Fig. 10
Drinking Cup

CUP AND SAUCER

1. Fold a square of paper diagonally both ways; undo.
2. Fold straight across both ways, undo, and lay flat. Then you have Fig. 11.
3. Fold along dotted line in Fig. 11, bringing *AD* to *BC*. Then you have Fig. 12. Do *not* undo.
4. Fold along dotted lines in Fig. 12. Do *not* undo, and you have Fig. 13.
5. Fold along dotted line in Fig. 13. Do *not* undo, and you get Fig. 14.
6. Pull out point *X* to the left (Fig. 15) and point *Y* to the right, and you have Fig. 16.

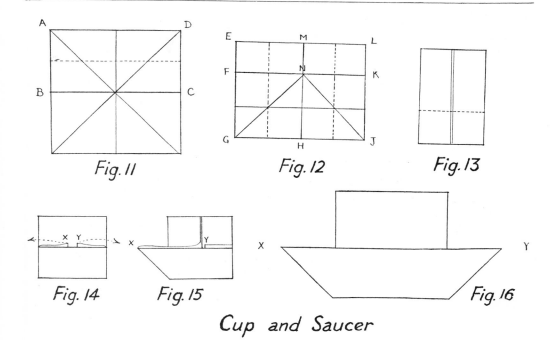

Fig. 11   Fig. 12   Fig. 13

Fig. 14   Fig. 15   Fig. 16

Cup and Saucer

WINDMILL

1. Fold a square of paper diagonally both ways; undo.
2. Fold the four corners to the centre and you have Fig. 17.
3. Fold along dotted lines bringing *AB* to the centre line *WX*, also the line *CD* to the centre line *WX*. Crease well, then undo both folds.
4. Fold *AC* to the centre line *YZ*, also fold *BD* to *YZ*. Crease well, undo, and you have Fig. 17.

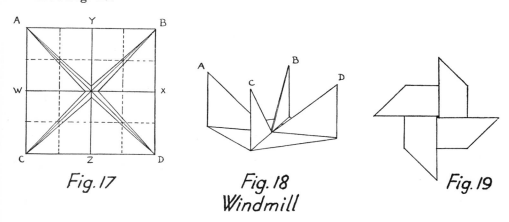

Fig. 17   Fig. 18   Fig. 19

Windmill

5. At this stage fold diagonally both ways and press well; undo.

6. Bring the centres of the four sides, *W*, *X*, *Y*, and *Z*, to the centre of the figure. This will cause the four corners, *A*, *B*, *C*, *D*, to stand up perpendicularly, as shown in Fig. 18.

7. Flatten each corner down in rotation, and all in the one direction and you have Fig. 19.

DUSTPAN

1. Fold a square of paper diagonally both ways; undo; lay flat.

2. Fold straight across in half both ways; undo.

3. Fold the four corners to the centre *E* and you have Fig. 20.

4. Fold along dotted lines, bringing *A*, *B*, and *C* to the centre line *DEF*, also bringing *GHI* to *DEF*. Undo.

5. Fold *ADG* to the centre line *BEH*, also *CFI* to *BEH*. Do *not* undo the last two folds, and you have Fig. 21.

6. Fold in half along *OP*. Undo, then fold along the dotted line *MJN*, which will bring *K* to *O* and *L* to *P*. Undo and lay back as it was.

7. Raise up *S* to *M*, folding along dotted line between *O* and *J*. Press heavily.

8. Raise up *T* to *N*, folding along dotted line between *P* and *J*, and press heavily between *J* and *P*. The last two folds will cause the portion above the line *OSTP* to stand erect.

9. Fold *KL* down to *OP*, enclosing the line *MJN*. Press this thick line heavily.

   O, *P*, *Q*, and *R* become the corners of the base, and the three sides stand up vertically as in Fig. 22.

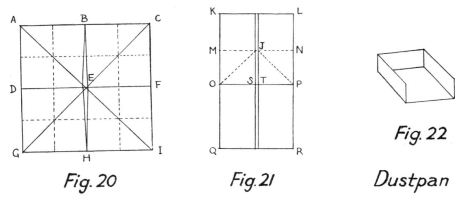

Fig. 20   Fig. 21   Fig. 22

Dustpan

DOLL'S BED

1. Fold a square of paper diagonally both ways; undo; lay flat.

2. Fold *A* and *C* to *E*.

3. Turn paper over and fold *B* and *D* to *E* on the other side.

4. Turn paper back again.

CHINESE LANTERN   BOX ON FOUR FEET   STAMP BOX
PAPER BASKET   TABLE AND GUESTS   UMBRELLA
DRINKING-CUP   PEN   KETTLE

PLATE I

5. Fold along dotted lines in Fig. 24, bringing *GF* to *HL*, also *JK* to *HL*, taking care that the folds cross the flaps as in diagram.

6. Turn figure over and lay flat, and you have Fig. 25.

7. Fold *MNOP* forward along dotted line to *STUV*.

8. Fold *C* (Fig. 26), top layer only, along *AF* to *G*.

9. Fold *D*, top layer only, to *H* along line *EB*.

10. Turn over and repeat on the other side.

11. Lay flat as in Fig. 27, and lift right up the points *Q* and *R*, at the same time bringing the margins together. As the model opens out again, *Q* and *R* make the head and foot of the bed.

12. The four corners *M*, *P*, *S*, and *V* become the feet, as shown in Fig. 28.

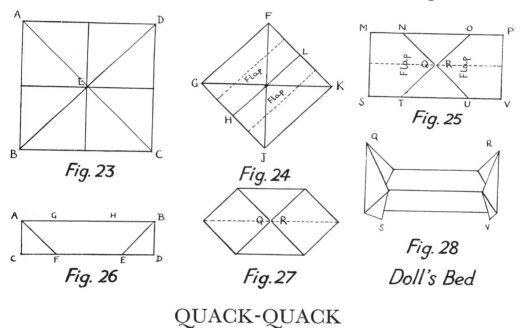

Fig. 23   Fig. 24   Fig. 25

Fig. 26   Fig. 27   Fig. 28 Doll's Bed

QUACK-QUACK

Take a piece of stiff paper 8 *in.* × 10 *in.*

1. Fold in half along dotted line in Fig. 29 and lay flat as shown in Fig. 30.

2. Fold in half again to get the centre line *BD*; undo.

3. Fold along dotted line, bringing *A* to the centre line. Also fold *C* to the centre line to meet *A*. Then you have Fig. 31.

4. Fold up the single margin *GHJ* along dotted line.

5. Turn over and repeat, and you have Fig. 32.

6. Open out where arrow points. Bring *L* and *M* together.

7. Lay flat and arrange corners as *O* in Fig. 33.

8. Do the same to corners on the other side.
9. Fold *O* up to *N*.
10. Turn figure over and repeat and you have Fig. 34.
11. Open again where arrow points.
12. Bring *P* to *Q* and lay flat as in Fig. 35.
13. Place *S* on *R*.

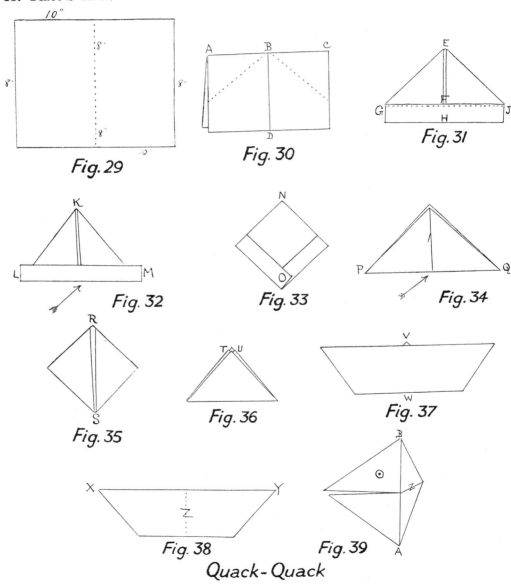

Fig. 29

Fig. 30

Fig. 31

Fig. 32

Fig. 33

Fig. 34

Fig. 35

Fig. 36

Fig. 37

Fig. 38

Fig. 39

Quack-Quack

14. Turn over and repeat and you have Fig. 36.
15. Draw *T* and *U* (the two side points) apart and you have Fig. 37.
16. To enclose the point *V* lift up the single flap between *V* and *W* and place point *V* under the flap, then replace the single flap again and you have Fig. 38.
17. The central line at *Z* and the corresponding line on the other side become the hinge. Open out along *XY* and bring *X* and *Y* together to make the duck's beak.
18. Add an eye each side.
19. Place your first and second fingers at *B* and your thumb at *A* and make the mouth open and shut in imitation of a duck quacking, and you have Fig. 39.

DART

Take an oblong piece of paper 8 in. × 10 in.

1. Fold in half from *B* to *D* to find the centre; undo.
2. Fold along the two dotted lines in Fig. 40, bringing *A* and *C* to *D*—Fig. 41.
3. Fold again along two dotted lines in Fig. 41, bringing *F* and *H* to *J*.

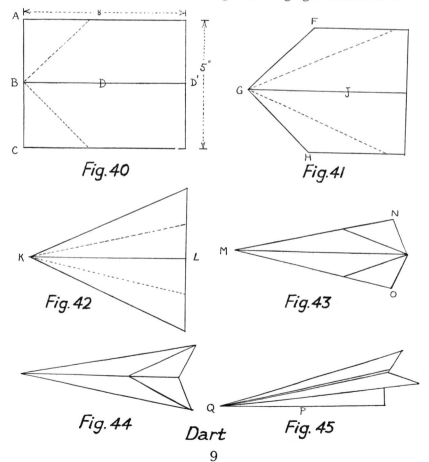

Fig. 40

Fig. 41

Fig. 42

Fig. 43

Fig. 44

Dart

Fig. 45

4. Turn figure over, and you have Fig. 42.
5. Fold again along two dotted lines to the centre line *KL* and you have Fig. 43.
6. Fold *N* backwards to *O*. Crease in half all the way along to *M*.
7. Turn figure right over and look below and you will find three folds.
8. Catch the centre one at the point *P* in Fig. 45 and spread out the two wings as shown in Fig. 44.

To throw dart hold fold on which *P* occurs, and aim in an upward arc.

PICNIC SALT CELLAR

1. Fold a square of paper diagonally both ways; undo.
2. Turn paper over and fold straight across in half both ways, undo, and lay flat.
3. Turn paper back again.
4. Fold all four corners to the centre and you have Fig. 46.
5. Turn paper over and fold all the corners to the centre again and you have Fig. 47.
6. Fold firmly along the lines *AB* and *CD* in Fig. 47. Undo.
7. Turn paper over and push up the centre from below.
8. Pull out all the single corners, *E, F, G, H,* from the flat surface in Fig. 48, so that *W, X, Y,* and *Z* form the feet of the salt cellar.

To make this fold easy, pinch along dotted lines in Fig. 48.

The salt cellar will then stand alone.

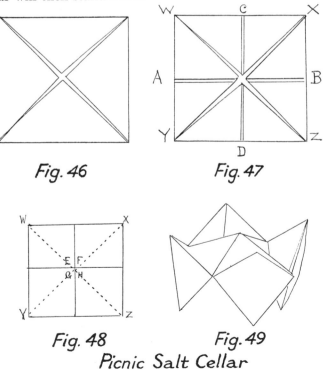

Fig. 46   Fig. 47

Fig. 48   Fig. 49

Picnic Salt Cellar

BOAT

1. Fold a square of paper diagonally both ways; undo.
2. Fold straight across in half both ways; undo.
3. Fold along all the dotted lines in Fig. 50; undo after each fold.
4. Use *EFGH* as your base, and bring *J*, *K*, *L*, and *M* together at the centre *I*. The four corners will then stand erect, bringing 1 to 2, 3 to 4, 5 to 6, and 7 to 8.
5. Lay down flat and arrange two corners up and two corners down as shown in Fig. 51.
6. Raise up *P* and fold upwards and to the left along dotted line *CX*.
7. Fold figure backwards along dotted line *AB*, Fig. 51.
8. Unfold *AXN*, to form the sail.

   P and *O* become the stern of the boat and *Q* is brought up to become the prow.
9. Fold *P* back round the sail, so that the point rests between the sail and *OQ*.

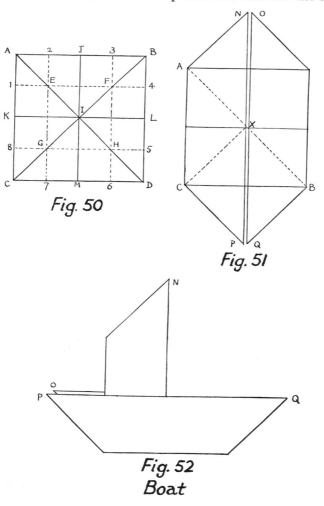

Fig. 50

Fig. 51

Fig. 52

Boat

THE PIG

1. Fold a 6 in. square of paper diagonally both ways; undo.
2. Turn paper over, and fold straight across in half both ways; undo; turn paper back again, lay flat.
3. Fold along dotted lines in Fig. 53, bringing *ABC* and *GFE* to the middle line *HD*; undo.
4. Fold *AHG* and *CDE* to the middle line *BF*, and you have Fig. 54.
5. Raise up point *J* and place it on *Q*, then press along dotted line *JA* shown in Fig. 54. This fold is shown partially done in Fig. 55.

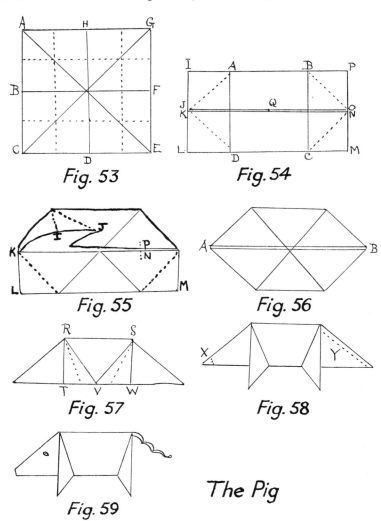

Fig. 53

Fig. 54

Fig. 55

Fig. 56

Fig. 57

Fig. 58

Fig. 59

The Pig

6. Raise up point *O*, place it on *Q*, and press along dotted line *OB*. Raise up *K*, place it on *Q*, and press along dotted line *KD*.

7. Raise up *N*, place *N* on *Q*, and press along dotted line *NC*.

8. Turn over and fold figure in half lengthways, along middle line, and you have Fig. 57.

9. Fold the line *RV* (top layer only) along dotted line to the line *RT*, and fold *SV*, top layer only, along dotted line to *SW*.

10. Turn over and do the same on the other side.

11. Cut along dotted line in Fig. 58 to make the pig's tail, and twist it round as in Fig. 59.

12. Tuck out of sight the triangular portions marked *Y* inside the pig's body.

13. Fold up the point *X* inside out of sight to make the pig's snout.

14. Add an eye, and you have Fig. 59.

FLOWER BASKET

This is made with two pieces of paper, each 6 in. square, one pink and the other mauve; these are folded together.

1. Fold the papers diagonally both ways; undo.

2. Fold each corner to the centre, and you have Fig. 60.

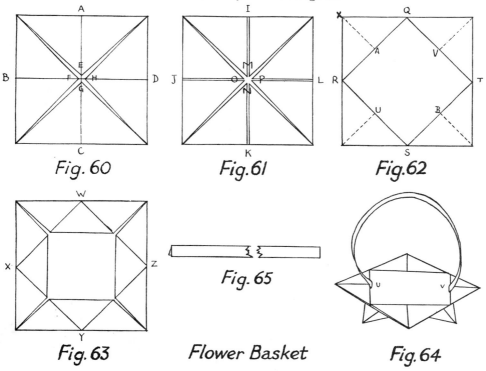

Fig. 60   Fig. 61   Fig. 62

Fig. 63   Flower Basket   Fig. 64

Fig. 65

3. Fold *E* to *A*, *F* to *B*, *G* to *C*, and *H* to *D*.
4. Turn figure over and fold the four corners to the centre again, and you have Fig. 61.
5. Fold *M* to *I*, *O* to *J*, *P* to *L*, and *N* to *K*, turn figure over again, and you have Fig. 62.
6. Pick up layer at *A*, pinch firmly along dotted line *AX*, bringing *R* and *Q* together.
7. Repeat at *V*, *B*, and *U*.
8. Fig. 63 shows the reverse side of the figure. The points *W*, *X*, *Y*, and *Z* become the four feet.
9. Cut a strip of paper $\frac{1}{2}$ in. × 5 in.
10. Fold it in half lengthwise and paste it together to make the handle stiff as shown in Fig. 65.
11. Fix one end inside *V* in Fig. 62, and the other end inside *U* in Fig. 62, and you have Fig. 64.

TEDDY BEAR

An oblong of paper 4 in. × 6½ in. makes two figures as shown in Fig. 68.

By folding many layers of paper long rows of bears may be cut out all in one piece. 4 in. × 13 in. makes four and so on.

1. Fold in half to get the centre line *CH*. Undo. Place the line *AF* on the centre line *CH*. Place the line *EK* on the line *CH*. Do not undo.
2. Fold backwards along the line *CH*, and you have Fig. 67.
3. See that you place it down properly. The two folds should be at the left-hand side, and the centre fold *CH*, with a single margin on each side, should be at the right-hand side.
4. Draw the half figure on the top surface only, and cut out through all the layers like Fig. 67.
5. Be careful not to cut at the point *O*, as the bears are held together only at the wrists.

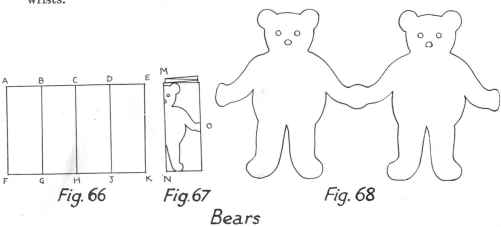

Fig. 66   Fig. 67   Fig. 68

Bears

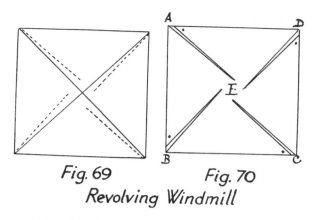

Fig. 69   Fig. 70

Revolving Windmill

REVOLVING WINDMILL

1. Fold a square of paper diagonally, both ways, and you have Fig. 69.
2. Cut along dotted lines in Fig. 69, and you have Fig. 70.
3. Pass a pin through dots in Fig. 70 at A, D, C, and B from behind, and in the order given, then through the centre E.
4. Stick the pin into the blunt end of a full-length pencil. Hold the pencil out in front of you, as you walk, and the windmill will revolve.

XMAS DECORATION

1. Fold a 6 in. square of paper straight across in half, and you have Fig. 71.
2. Fold A to B and D to C.
3. Turn over and repeat, and you have Fig. 72.
4. You now have four layers. Arrange them so that you have the central double fold between G and H, with a single layer on each side of it. You will then have two double folds at the top.
5. Cut along as shown in Fig. 72 every $\frac{1}{4}$ in. between G and H, to within $\frac{1}{4}$ in. of the top line.

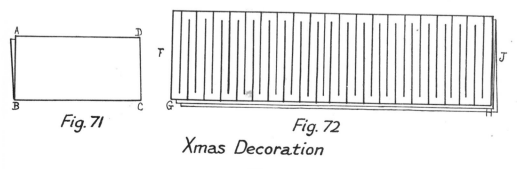

Fig. 71   Fig. 72

Xmas Decoration

6. Turn figure round, and cut from the opposite side, exactly between the first cuts, to within ¼ in. of the line *GH*.

7. Keep figure folded, and carefully undo the three folds across lengthwise, and lay flat in its original square. This is important, or it may become entangled.

8. Draw *F* and *J* gently apart and you will have a festoon about a yard in length.

Any one with a straight eye can gauge where to cut without measuring, and thus save time in making decorations.

KING'S CROWN

This requires a piece of paper 6 in. square.

1. Fold it diagonally both ways; undo.

2. Turn paper over, and fold straight across in half both ways; undo.

3. Turn paper back again.

4. Fold each corner to the centre, and you have Fig. 73. Do *not* undo.

5. Turn figure over, and fold each corner to the centre again.

6. Turn paper back, and you have Fig. 74.

7. Bring *A* and *B* together, by folding forward along dotted line in Fig. 74, and you have Fig. 75.

8. Undo and lay flat like Fig. 74.

9. Pinch up both dotted lines in Fig. 74, one layer only, between finger and thumb of each hand, bringing *A* and *B* together, and you have Fig. 76.

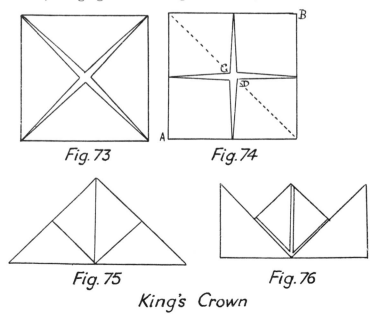

Fig. 73   Fig. 74

Fig. 75   Fig. 76

King's Crown

BOOK MARK

1. Cut an oblong piece of paper like Fig. 77, $1\frac{1}{4}$ in. $\times$ 6 in.
2. Fold in half along dotted line in Fig. 77, and you have Fig. 78.
3. Cut along the folded edge in a slanting way about every $\frac{1}{2}$ in. apart, like Fig. 78. Undo and lay flat.
4. Fold back each point as in Fig. 79, along dotted lines like *AB* in Fig. 78.
5. Paste a piece of paper of a contrasting colour behind, to show through the open spaces. Make this large enough to leave a $\frac{1}{4}$ in. margin all round, as in Fig. 79.
6. A variation may be made by cutting every $\frac{1}{4}$ in. in Fig. 78, then folding back every alternate point into the small opening between the points. Interlace a very narrow piece of paper $\frac{1}{8}$ in. wide and paste all down on the background leaving a margin all round.
    The narrow lacing paper may introduce a third colour. A little ingenuity will suggest other variations.

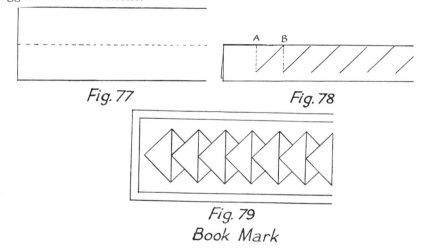

Fig. 77   *Fig. 78*

Fig. 79
Book Mark

TO PLAIT PAPER FOR HATS

For the sake of illustration I will use coloured paper streamers; the different colours will help the descriptions. I have taken four colours: green, fawn, blue, and pink. You simply make a foursome plait; but being of paper, it must be folded into angles at the corners, to make it lie flat.

$\frac{1}{4}$ in. $\times$ 10 in. is a convenient size to work with; but as you do not want the joins to come all at one place, cut your first pieces of different lengths, and make the overlap about $\frac{3}{4}$ in. at the joins. Cut 4 in., 6 in., 8 in., and 10 in. After the first, they should all be 10 in. You must hide the joins underneath, so that they do not show on the hat.

1. Fix ends down with drawing-pins and interlace strips as shown in Fig. 80. The angle between the two sets of strips should be 60°.

2. To begin the plaiting, bend the Blue back under the Green at *B*, and up over the Fawn. The Blue should now be in the position shown by the dotted lines in Fig. 80. If the Blue strip is not in this position, alter the angles of the strips so that it is so, as the success of the plait depends on this first bend. Having arranged this, bend back the Blue strip under the Pink, and it should lie next to the Fawn again, only on the lower side. This is another check on a correct start.

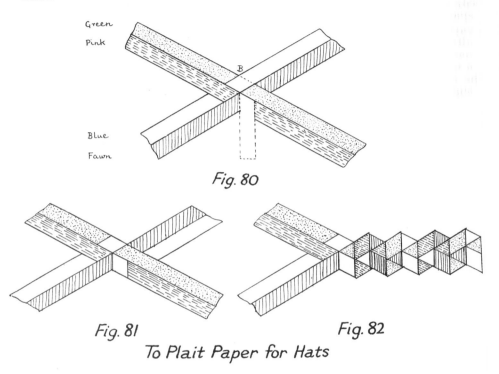

Fig. 80

Fig. 81   *Fig. 82*

To Plait Paper for Hats

3. Bend the Pink back under the Blue, carry it under the Blue and over the Green and bend back round the Fawn.

4. Bend the Fawn back round the Pink and carry it under the Pink and over the Blue, and bend it back to enclose the Green.

5. Bend the Green back round the Fawn and bring it up over the Pink, bend the Green back round the Blue and over the Fawn.

6. Repeat from Para. 2.

   The natives of South Africa make hats in this way from mealie sheaths (the outer covering of maize) torn into narrow strips.

   Cut 1 in. × 20 in. of crinkled paper, fold in $\frac{1}{4}$ in. along each side, then double in half lengthwise, and you have $\frac{1}{4}$ in. strips to plait with. This can be sewn round and round, and shaped into hats.

FAN

1. Fold a square of paper diagonally once only, like Fig. 83.
2. Fold along dotted line in Fig. 83, bringing *A* to *B*.
3. Fold in half once more (being careful to keep the centre marked *X*, always in the centre), and you have Fig. 84.
4. Fold along dotted line bringing *D* to *E* in Fig. 84, and you have Fig. 85. Press heavily as you now have sixteen layers of paper folded together.
5. Cut along dotted scallops, undo, and lay flat.
6. Fold the circle in half and arrange folds backwards and forwards alternately, making an inverted fold on each dotted line in Fig. 86.
7. The fan should be double with sixteen scallops.
8. Fasten a strip of paper of a contrasting colour round the centre to form a handle at *F* in Fig. 86.

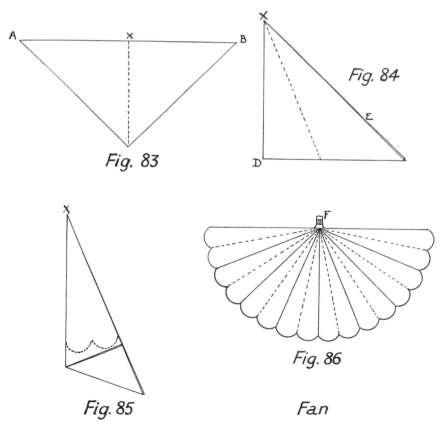

Fig. 83

Fig. 84

Fig. 85

Fig. 86

Fan

LANTERN

1. Cut a piece of paper 5 in. × 2½ in.
2. Fold in half lengthwise like Fig. 87.
3. Cut along the folded layer every ¼ in. in a slanting direction, as shown in Fig. 87.
4. Undo the centre fold and lay flat as in Fig. 88. Join into a circle, by pasting *ABC* on to *FED*.
5. Cut another piece of paper of a contrasting colour 5 in. × 2 in. and paste it inside the circle, joining it from *A* to *F* at the top, and from *C* to *D* below. This will cause the outer circle to bulge at the centre and look like Fig. 89.
6. Make a handle by twisting strips of the two colours together to match the lantern, and paste to the centre of each side of the lantern.

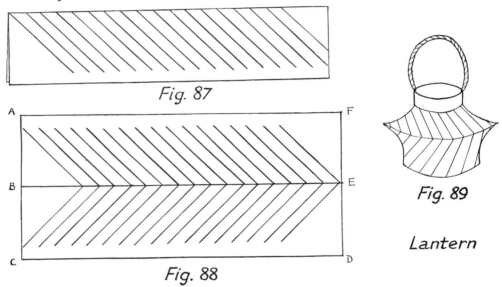

Fig. 87

Fig. 88

Fig. 89

Lantern

HAT

The hat requires an oblong piece of paper 18 in. × 24 in. to make a hat for a child.

1. Fold along dotted line in Fig. 90. Be careful to put the fold in the longest **way** of the paper.
2. Lay figure down as shown in Fig. 91.
3. Fold in half again, to get the centre *BD*; undo.
4. Fold along dotted lines bringing the line *AB* down along the centre *BD* also bringing the line *BC* down along *BD*, and you have Fig. 92.
5. Fold *FGH* up along dotted line, one layer only.
6. Turn figure over and repeat.

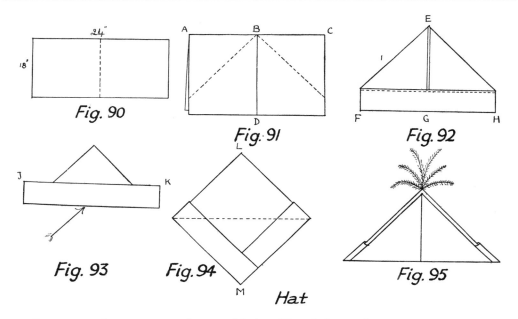

Fig. 90 Fig. 91 Fig. 92

Fig. 93 Fig. 94 Fig. 95

Hat

7. Open out where arrow points and bring *K* and *J* together.
8. Lay flat and adjust the corners as shown in Fig. 94.
9. Turn over and repeat.
10. Fold *M* to *L* along dotted line.
11. Turn over and repeat.
12. Make a small hole at *L* and insert strips of paper of contrasting colour cut to represent feathers, and you have Fig. 95.

BOAT

1. Cut a piece of paper 5 in. × 4 in.
2. Fold along dotted line to get the centre placing *AC* on *BD*. This paper is oblong, so be careful to make the fold across the longest way of the paper.
3. Lay figure down as shown in Fig. 97.
4. Fold in half again to get the centre, undo last fold.
5. Fold along dotted lines bringing *E* and *G* to the centre line, and you have Fig. 98.
6. Fold the single margin *HJ* up along dotted line.
7. Turn over and do the same on the other side and you have Fig. 99.
8. Open out where arrow points, bringing *H* and *J* together. Lay flat and arrange corners on both sides, back and front, as shown in Fig. 100.
9. Fold along dotted line, top layer only.
10. Turn over and do the same on the other side.

11. Open out as in Fig. 99 and bring *I* and *K* together, and you have Fig. 101.
12. Fold along dotted line, top layer only.
13. Turn over and do the same on the other side and you have Fig. 102.
14. Draw *L* and *M* apart, and you have Fig. 103.

The addition of two gaily coloured flags, as shown in Fig. 103, adds greatly to the appearance of this boat.

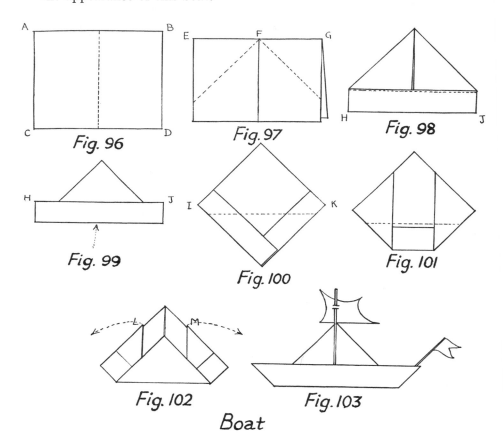

Fig. 96

Fig. 97

Fig. 98

Fig. 99

Fig. 100

Fig. 101

Fig. 102

Fig. 103

Boat

LADDER

This requires thin and tough paper. Cut it 6 in. × 10 in.

1. Roll, not too tightly, round a pencil, the narrow way (6 in. way) of the paper.
2. Slip pencil out. Press it flat.
3. Cut along the roll as shown in Fig. 104, removing the shaded portion marked *ABCD*, which is half the width of the roll, and one-third of the length.

4. By flattening the roll in the opposite way, the inside of the roll will be uppermost, and it will be easy then to turn *E* down at *AB*, and *F* down at *DC*, as shown in Fig. 105.

5. Let one person hold the portion *G* in the left hand and *H* in the right hand, while you gently pull the top layer of the paper at *J*, straight up, and the coils inside *G* and *H* will come up and form Fig. 106.

Paste corners at *J* and *K* to prevent unrolling.

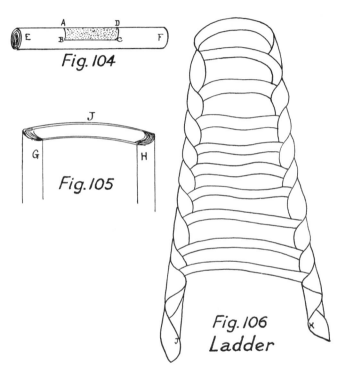

Fig. 104

Fig. 105

Fig. 106
Ladder

STORK

1. Fold a square of paper straight across in half both ways; undo.

2. Turn paper over and fold diagonally both ways; undo (see Fig. 107). Turn over. hold *C* down with forefinger, and place *D* and *B* on *C*. At the same time, press *A* on to *DB* and *C* and you have Fig. 108. With the four points towards you, fold down in half to get the centre line. Undo.

3. Fold along dotted line *MN* by bringing *E* down on to centre line; undo.

4. Lift up *G* beyond *E*, bend it upwards at *NM*, and place it at *L* in Fig. 109.

5. Press down the margins *JL* and *KL* to meet each other and make the triangles *LMJ* and *LKN*.

6. Turn over and repeat, and you have Fig. 110.

7. Lay flat with the two divided points next to you, one to the left and one to the right.

8. Fold along dotted lines, bringing *O* to *P* and *Q* to *P*, single layer only.

9. Turn over and repeat, and you have Fig. 111.

10. Raise point *T* to the left (inverting the middle fold) along the dotted line between *S* and *V* to make the stork's breast.

11. Fold along dotted line at *R*, inverting the middle fold, to make the head.

12. For a flying stork fold between *V* and *W*, and raise *U* to *X*.

13. For a walking stork open out *WU* and cut up the centre *U* to *V*.

14. Turn up ½ in. to make feet at *Y*, inverting the middle fold.

15. Draw down the wings and flatten the back; add eyes.

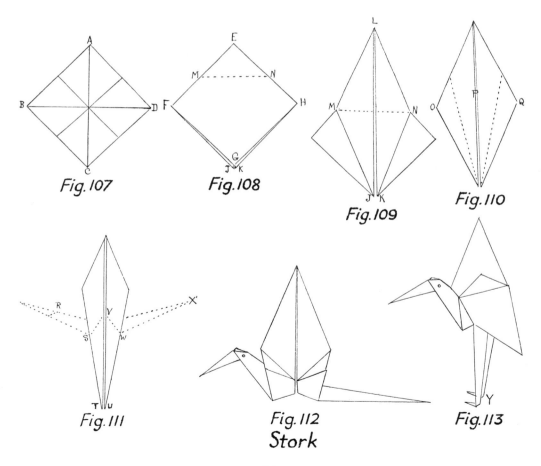

Fig. 107

Fig. 108

Fig. 109

Fig. 110

Fig. 111

Fig. 112
Stork

Fig. 113

CLOSED BOX

1. Fold a square of paper diagonally both ways; undo.

2. Fold in half both ways; undo.

3. Fold each corner to the centre along dotted lines in Fig. 114, undo, lay flat and you have Fig. 115.

4. Fold along dotted lines in Fig. 115, fold *A* to *G* and *B* to *H*, fold *C* to *E*, and *D* to *F*, undo after each fold, lay flat and you have Fig. 116.

5. Fold along dotted lines, and bring *J* to *N*, undo, *M* to *O*, undo, *K* to *P*, undo, and *L* to *Q*, undo, lay flat and you have Fig. 117.

6. Cut along dotted lines with sharp scissors *R* to *S* in Fig. 117, and from *T* to *U*, also from *W* to *V*, and from *Y* to *X*.

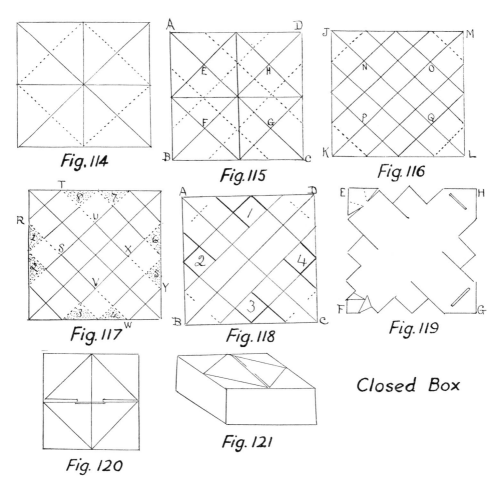

Fig. 114

Fig. 115

Fig. 116

Fig. 117

Fig. 118

Fig. 119

Fig. 120

Fig. 121

Closed Box

7. Remove all the shaded triangles surrounded by dotted lines, marked 1, 2, 3, 4, 5, 6, 7, 8, and you have Fig. 119.

8. At corners *A* and *D* in Fig. 118, cut slots where dotted lines indicate (like corner *H* in Fig. 119) and on the opposite corners *C* and *B* cut in, on each side, as dotted lines show, to near the centre, to make a fastener which will go through the slot (see corner *E* in Fig. 119).

9. On corner *F*, Fig. 119, you will see how to bend the corners, to let them pass through the slot.

10. Fig. 120 shows how to arrange the corner once it is through—

11. To close the box put corner *F* in Fig. 119, through the slot at *H*, closing flaps at 1, 2, 3, 4, in Fig. 118, on each side, then finish by fastening *E*, folded like *F* in Fig. 119 through the slot at *G*, Fig. 119. Flatten out bent corners, and you have Fig. 121.

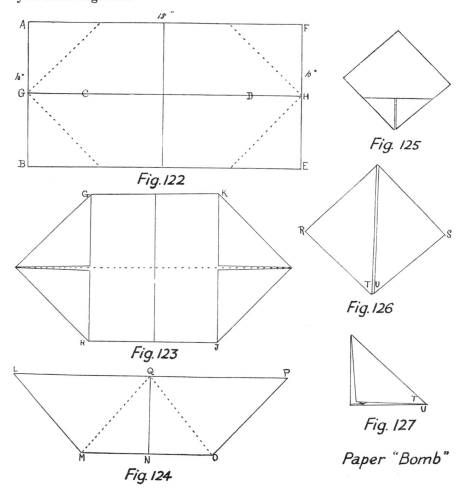

Fig. 122

Fig. 123

Fig. 124

Fig. 125

Fig. 126

Fig. 127

Paper "Bomb"

PAPER "BOMB"

1. Take a *stiff* piece of paper 10 in. × 18 in. Brown paper does well.
2. Fold in half lengthwise, undo; also fold across, undo, and you have Fig. **122**.
3. Fold *AG* along the line *GC*, also fold *BG* along the line *GC*, do the same to the other end, and you have Fig. **123**.
4. Fold along dotted line, and you have Fig. **124**.
5. Fold in half, bringing *L* to *P*, to get the centre line; undo.
6. Fold along the dotted lines, bringing the line *QL* along the line *QN*, also the line *QP* along the line *QN*, and you have Fig. **126**. (Fig. **125** shows reverse side.)
7. Fold *R* to *S* backwards. Now your figure is doubled up in half as shown in Fig. **127**.
8. Catch the points *T* and *U* together, by the forefinger and thumb of your right hand, raise your hand high above your head, and with a quick downward throw of your arm, it ought to go off with the noise of a bomb.

PURSE

1. Cut a piece of rather stiff paper 6 in. × 10 in., Fig. **128**.
2. Fold along centre dotted line, bringing *AD* to *BC*; undo and lay flat.
3. Fold along corner dotted lines, bringing *A* and *B* to *E*, and *D* and *C* to *G*, and you have Fig. **129**.

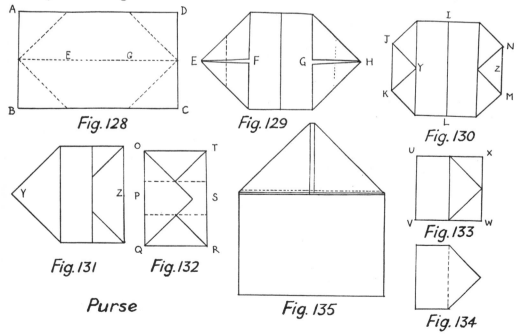

Fig. 128   Fig. 129   Fig. 130

Fig. 131   Fig. 132   Fig. 133

Purse   Fig. 135   Fig. 134

4. Fold *E* to *H* to get the centre line; undo and lay flat.
5. Fold *E* to *F* and *H* to *G* along dotted lines, and you have Fig. 130.
6. Fold the line *JK* to the centre line *IL*, undo both folds, see Fig. 131, and also fold the line *NM* to the centre *IL*, do not undo and you have Fig. 131.
7. Place *Y* on to *Z* section to form the lap-over of the purse, as shown in Fig. 132.
8. Fold backwards along the two dotted lines, and you have Fig. 133.
9. Fold *XW* backwards to *UV*, and you have Fig. 134.
10. Fold along dotted line and push the top point in Fig. 135 into the front pocket of the purse.

THE CICADA

1. Fold a square of paper diagonally both ways; undo, and you have Fig. 136.
2. Fold *A* to *B*, and you have Fig. 137.
3. Fold *C* to *D* and *E* to *D*, and you have Fig. 138.
4. Fold *G* to *F* and *H* to *F*, single layers only, and you have Fig. 139.
5. Fold along dotted lines, single layers only, taking *J* to *L* and *K* to *M*.
6. Now turn figure right over and fold *N* to *O* also *P* to *O*, then fold *Q* up to *R*, and you have Fig. 141.
7. Turn figure over again, and add eyes at the corners.

POPLAR TREE

This requires a length of green paper 2½ in. × 10 in. wide.

1. Roll up tightly round a pencil till all the paper is used up.
2. Remove the pencil from the centre.
3. Cut down about ¾ in. at the four places on the roll marked *A*, *B*, *C*, and *D*.
4. Fix the end *E* with paste and prevent it unrolling, then gently pull up from the centre of the roll where arrow points to form the tree, and you have Fig. 144.
5. Roll green silk tightly round the trunk between *F* and *G*.

PALM TREE

This requires a strip of green tissue paper 20 in. × 5 in., but it is easier to do it with two strips 10 in. × 5 in. each.

1. Double the paper in half lengthwise, then cut along the double edge in strips of ⅛ in. apart, as shown in Fig. 145 to within ½ in. of the two margins.

28

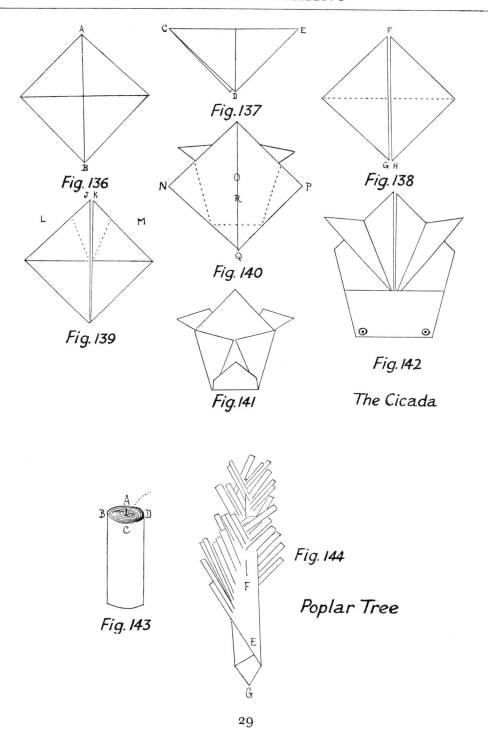

Fig. 136

Fig. 137

Fig. 138

Fig. 139

Fig. 140

Fig. 141

Fig. 142

The Cicada

Fig. 143

Fig. 144

Poplar Tree

2. Roll this round a pencil, beginning at the end *A*, and continue rolling till the whole length is used up. Roll straight at first and then roll spirally, and your tree will look natural.

3. Slip it gently off the pencil and bind with brown silk to make the stem.

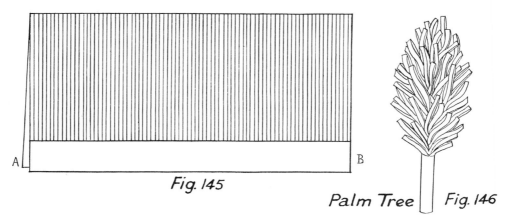

Fig. 145

Palm Tree   Fig. 146

AEROPLANE

1. Take a piece of paper 6 in. × 8 in. Cut off a square 6 in. × 6 in. and reserve the remainder to make the tail.

2. Fold the 6 in. square diagonally both ways, undoing after each fold.

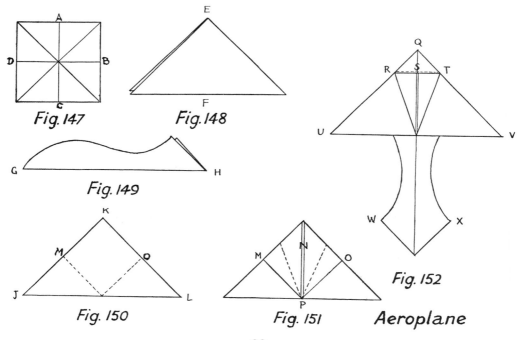

Fig. 147   Fig. 148

Fig. 149

Fig. 150   Fig. 151   Fig. 152

Aeroplane

3. Fold straight across in half once only; undo.

4. Turn paper over, and make the other straight fold in half; undo.

5. Reverse the paper again, and you have Fig. 147. *DB* is the fold made in para. 4.

6. Lift up *B* and *D* and bring down together on to *C*. *A* will now come over on top of *D*, *B*, and *C*, and you have Fig. 148. (This shows the use of the inverted fold.)

7. Fold along the dotted lines, Fig. 150, top layers only, bringing *J* and *L* to *K*, and you have Fig. 151.

8. Fold along dotted lines in Fig. 151, bringing *M* to *N* and *O* to *N* as in top section of Fig. 152.

9. Fold the tail piece in half lengthwise, cut out as in Fig. 149, and open out. Insert the point *G* into the slot *UV*, right up to *Q* in Fig. 152.

10. With sharp scissors cut all layers from *Q* to *S*. The points thus formed must be folded along dotted lines and pushed into the slots between *R* and *S*, and between *S* and *T*, till they entirely disappear (these slots are formed by the top fold).

11. Fold *U* on *V* and *W* on *X* backwards. To fly, throw in an upward arc.

UMBRELLA

1. Fold a square of paper straight across both ways; undo.

2. Fold diagonally both ways, open out, and you have Fig. 153.

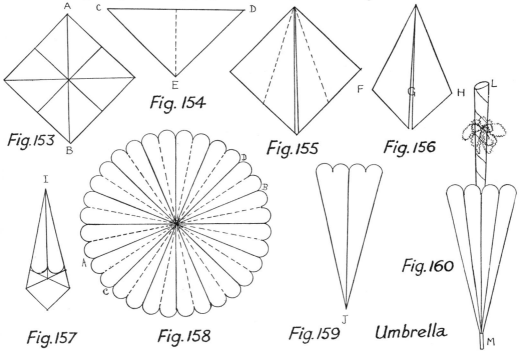

Fig. 153

Fig. 154

Fig. 155

Fig. 156

Fig. 157

Fig. 158

Fig. 159

Fig. 160

Umbrella

3. Fold *A* to *B*, and you have Fig. 154.

4. Fold along dotted line in Fig. 154 to get the centre; undo.

5. Fold *C* to *E* and *D* to *E*, and you have Fig. 155.

6. Fold backwards along dotted lines, and you have Fig. 156.

7. Fold *F* and *H* to *G*, and you have Fig. 157.

8. You have now sixteen layers on each side. Draw two scallops (see Fig. 157). Cut along the scallops through all thicknesses. Cut a small hole at *I*, Fig. 157.

9. Unfold the figure and lay flat, and pleat alternately up and down (see Fig. 158). The dotted lines show down folds and the black lines up folds. The best way to do this is to fold along each of the diagonal lines, e.g. along *AB* and *CD*, all the way round, then turn over and do the same along all the dotted lines (see Fig. 159).

10. To make the handle, roll up a strip of paper 1 in. × 5 in. in a slanting direction. Fix with paste. Put paste inside hole at *J* and insert the handle and you have Fig. 160.

Put paste along the pleatings to make them adhere to the stick, inside.

N.B. The directions for making the accordion pleating to decorate the handle will be found on page 51.

Note. A little ingenuity with silk and a weighty bead will turn this into a parachute, but for this the hole at *I* in Fig. 157 must be omitted.

LILY

1. Fold a square of paper straight across in half both ways; undo.

2. Turn paper over and fold diagonally both ways; undo and you have Fig. 161.

3. Push centre up from below and, by means of the inverted pleats, the four corners will come together. Fold and lay flat with the four corners towards you and two layers on each side, and you have Fig. 162.

4. Raise up *C* in Fig. 162 to stand vertically. It will have two single edges next to you.

5. Insert a pointed pencil between the edges right up to *A* and bring the line *AC* (Fig. 162) down directly over the centre line *AB*, and you have Fig. 163.

6. Turn over and repeat from para. 4.

7. Place *E* on *D*, then raise up the right-hand corner to the vertical position, and treat it exactly as you did *C* in Fig. 162.

8. Turn over and repeat, and you have Fig. 164.

9. Turn over one layer *G* to *I*. Repeat on the other side, and you should have a plain surface top and bottom, four corners next to you and four layers on each side.

10. Raise *H* up to *F*, and hold the points *H* and *F* firmly together while you place the single margin *MJ* along the centre line *JL* in Fig. 165.

11. It is necessary to insert a pencil where arrows point to manipulate and lay flat the angles which form at *X* in Fig. 166.

12. Now fold the margin *KJ* in Fig. 165 along the centre line *JL* as you did *MJ*.

13. Turn over and repeat.

14. Open out centre of sides, lay flat, and repeat the process on the two remaining sides, and you have Fig. 167.

15. Fold *P* down as far as it will go beyond *Q*, turn over and do the same on the other side.

16. Open out the centre on each side, and repeat with the other two surfaces, and you have Fig. 168.

17. Fold *U* to *T* single layer, turn over and repeat.

18. Turn figure upside down with the four points away from you—Fig. 169.

19. Fold along dotted lines, single layer, bringing *Y* and *Z* to the centre. Turn over and repeat. Open out the centre of the sides and repeat. Lay flat and you have Fig. 170.

20. Each petal must now be curled round a pencil as far as it will roll, and you have Fig. 171 (see also Plate II).

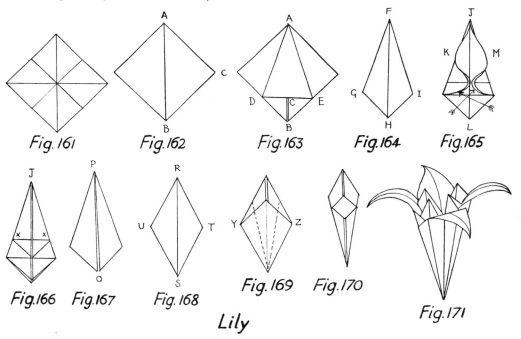

Fig. 161   Fig. 162   Fig. 163   Fig. 164   Fig. 165

Fig. 166   Fig. 167   Fig. 168   Fig. 169   Fig. 170   Fig. 171

Lily

SNAKE

1. Cut two long strips of green paper ½ in. wide.

2. Lay one out flat, and place the other over it at right angles, as in Fig. 172.

3. Fold *A* to *D*, and *B* to *C*, and you have Fig. 173.

4. Fold *G* to *E* and *H* to *F*.

5. Continue to fold each end alternately over the other, till the paper is used up, as shown in Fig. 174.

6. Make a head, eyes, and fangs at one end, taper the paper off to make a tail at the other, and you have Fig. 175.

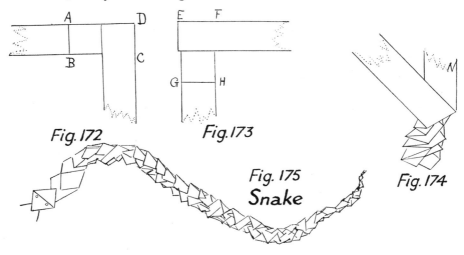

Fig. 172

Fig. 173

Fig. 175
Snake

Fig. 174

ENVELOPE

1. Cut a piece of paper 6 in. square. Fold it diagonally both ways, undoing after each fold.

2. Measure along one margin with a foot-rule and with a pencil mark exactly where 2 in. and 4 in. come (Fig. 176, L and K).

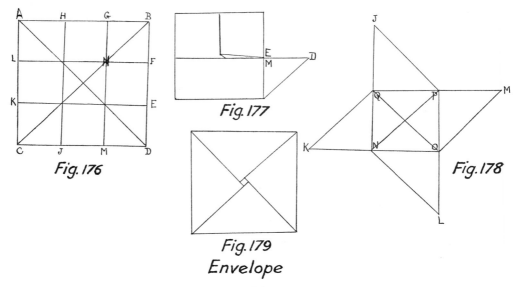

Fig. 176

Fig. 177

Fig. 178

Fig. 179
Envelope

3. Fold the line *CD* up to the line *LF* and bring *AB* down over that fold to the line *KE*. Undo and lay flat.

4. (See Fig. 176.) Fold the line *BD* to the line *HJ* and on top of that fold *AC* to the line *GM*. Undo and lay flat.

5. Fold *BD* to *HJ*.

6. Fold *CM* to *LN*. Pull out point *D* (Fig. 176), as shown in Fig. 177. Undo.

7. Do the same to the other three corners, undo, and lay flat.

8. When all are folded, bring *M* and *E* together between the forefinger and thumb of your right hand, and catch *L* and *H* (Fig. 176) together in the finger and thumb of your left hand. Twist the left hand towards you, and the right hand away from you, and the figure will fall into place, like Fig. 178.

9. Place *J* on *N*, *K* on *O*, *L* on *P*, and *M* must be pushed over *L* and under *JP* to *Q* to unlock it, and you then have Fig. 179.

THE HARLEQUIN STAMP BOX

1. Make six envelopes (page 34) in different colours and cut along the dotted lines, shown in Fig. 180, on the plain side, one layer only, and you will unfold four flaps, as in Fig. 181.

2. Do the same to all six envelopes.

3. Place four in a row. Paste the triangles together, to form four sides of a box. Add one envelope for the top and one for the bottom, and you have Fig. 182.

4. Label all the receptacles, on the outside of the square, with the value of the stamps enclosed—½d., 1d., 1½d., 2d., 2½d., 3d.

The stamps are placed in the centre of the square *QNOP*, as shown in Fig. 178 (the envelope) and the four points *J*, *K*, *L*, *M* are closed in rotation as described in para. 9, above). Repeat on all six surfaces, enclosing the six stamps.

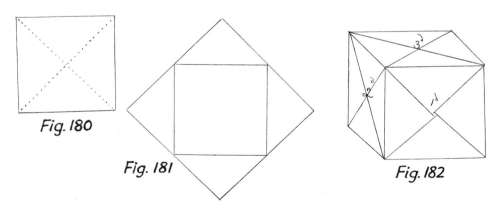

Fig. 180

Fig. 181

Fig. 182

The Harlequin Stamp Box

DUCK

1. Fold a square of stiff paper straight in half both ways; undo.

2. Turn paper over and fold diagonally both ways, undo, and you have Fig. 183.

3. Push the centre *E* up and bring the corners *A, B, C, D* together. Lay flat on the table with four single corners at the bottom *G*, and you have Fig. 185.

4. Fold *G* to *F* along dotted line in Fig. 185, one layer only.

5. Turn over and do the same on the other side, and you have Fig. 184.

6. Fold along dotted lines, single layer only, bringing *H* to *K* and *J* to *K*.

7. Turn over and repeat, and you have Fig. 186.

8. Open up where arrow points and fold point *M* up, inverting the centre line. Lay flat like Fig. 187.

9. Bend down where arrow points, inverting the centre line again to make head, and you have Fig. 188.

10. Treat the point *N* in the same way to make the tail, but only making the first bend, and you have Fig. 189.

11. *O* and *P* make the wings. Pull one down on each side.

12. Inflate by blowing into the opening at *Q*, and you have Fig. 190.

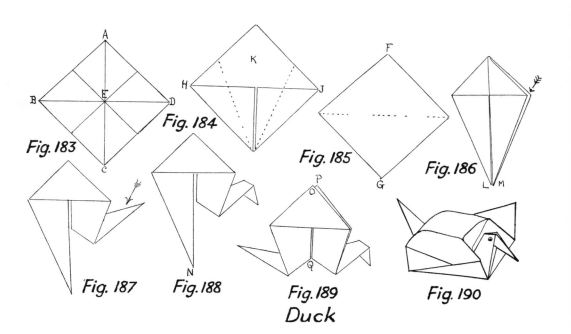

Fig. 183

Fig. 184

Fig. 185

Fig. 186

Fig. 187

Fig. 188

Fig. 189

Fig. 190

Duck

BUTTERFLY

This requires two squares of paper of different shades of the same colour, one slightly larger than the other.

1. Fold the squares in half diagonally; undo.

2. Take one square and fold every half-inch as shown in Fig. 191, in alternate directions, till the whole square is folded up and looks like Fig. 192. The diagonal fold line is a check to straight folding.

3. Do the same to the second square.

4. When finished, fasten both pieces together by tying tightly round the centre with strong silk, and you have Fig. 193.

5. Spread out the wings and join *A* to *B* with paste.

6. Add antennae.

Prettily coloured stamens used for centres of artificial flowers are best for antennae, but an inch of thick cotton, dipped, both ends, in sealing-wax will do.

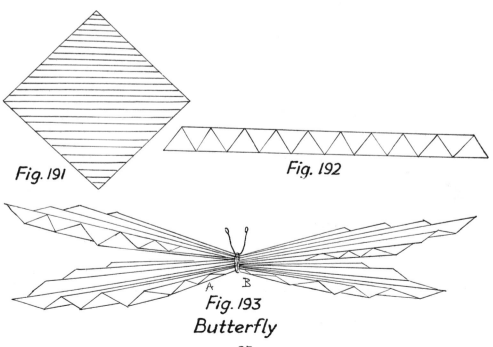

Fig. 191   Fig. 192

Fig. 193
Butterfly

PLAITED BELT

Decorative paper-tape or leather makes a nice belt. Tape is sold in reels $\frac{1}{2}$ in. wide and 12 in. long.

1. Cut leather or paper into strips $\frac{1}{2}$ in. $\times$ $4\frac{1}{4}$ in. as shown in Fig. 194.
2. Fold in half at dotted line *AC*, and undo.
3. Fold *B* to line *AC*, also *D* to the line *AC*, and you have Fig. 195.
4. Fold the line *EF* to the line *HG*. Make several pieces exactly like this, before beginning to plait. Fig. 196 shows the second piece.
5. Push the end marked *EF* of the first piece into the double slot at *LM* in the second piece, from below.
6. Push the end marked *HG* of the first piece into the slot at *JK* in the second piece. Push both the ends right up as shown in Fig. 197 at *O*.
7. Thread the next folded piece through the two slots at *PQ* in the same way.
8. Repeat till the belt is long enough and it should look like Fig. 198.
9. Finish off with a buckle.

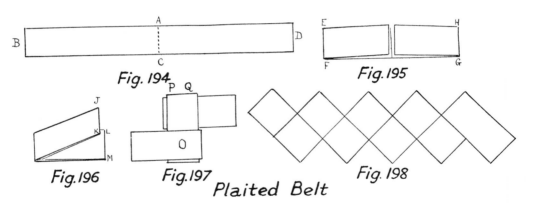

Fig. 194 Fig. 195 Fig. 196 Fig. 197 Fig. 198

Plaited Belt

JAPANESE HELMET

1. Fold a square of paper diagonally both ways, undo after each fold, and you have Fig. 199.
2. Fold along dotted line bringing *C* to *B*, and you have Fig. 200.
3. Fold along dotted line bringing *F* down to *G* (that is where *C* was in Fig. 199), and you have Fig. 201.
4. Fold along dotted lines in Fig. 201, bringing *H* and *J* to *K*, and you have Fig. 202.
5. Place *L* on *K*, top layer only, also *M* on *K*, along dotted line in Fig. 202, and you have Fig. 203.
6. Fold top layer along dotted lines in Fig. 203, and you have Fig. 204.

7. Fold Q to P, and you have Fig. 205. Pencil in the dotted lines and letters.

8. Fold R (one layer only) right down across dotted line WZ. This will bring the line Va down to XY.

9. Leave Va on XY and fold R up again, which brings the line Ub along the line WZ.

10. Fold R down again across the dotted line Ub, placing the line Tc along XY.

11. Leave Tc on XY and fold R up again and place the line Sd along the line WZ.

12. Fold R down again to the centre of the line XY, and you have Fig. 206.

NOTE. If you make the helmet of two squares, red and yellow, folded together as one throughout, it looks well.

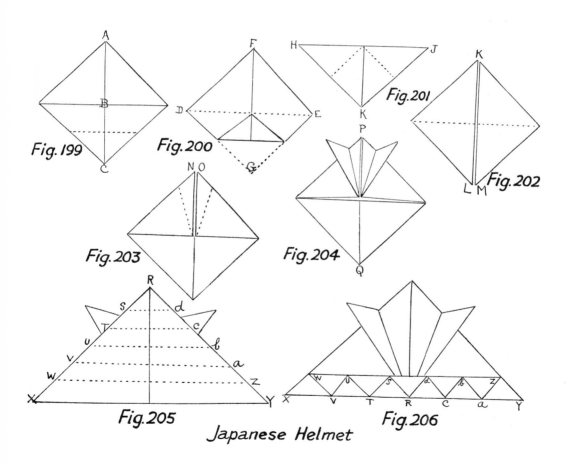

Fig. 199

Fig. 200

Fig. 201

Fig. 202

Fig. 203

Fig. 204

Fig. 205

Fig. 206

Japanese Helmet

LOVER'S KNOT

1. Fold a square of paper diagonally both ways, undo, and lay flat.

2. Fold all the corners to the centre, and you have Fig. 207.

3. Turn figure over and fold all the corners to the centre again.

4. Turn figure over again, and you have Fig. 208.

5. Pinch up the four dotted lines, top layer only, which will bring *A* and *D* together, also *A* and *B* together, on the left, and *C* and *B*, also *C* and *D*, together on the right; lay flat, and you have Fig. 209.

6. Open up where arrows point, and bring *E* (top layer) to *G*, and also *F* (top layer) to *G*, and you have Fig. 210.

7. Turn over and do the same on the other side, and you have Fig. 211.

8. Fold *H* to *J* top layer only, along dotted line.

9. Fold *L* to *K*, top layer only.

10. Turn over and do the same on the other side, and you have Fig. 212.

11. Catch all the bottom layers of the figure at *M*, in your right hand, leaving the centre free, and catch all the top layers in your left hand.

12. Hold each tightly, and draw gently apart, at the same time pushing up the centre point behind, and you will have Fig. 213.

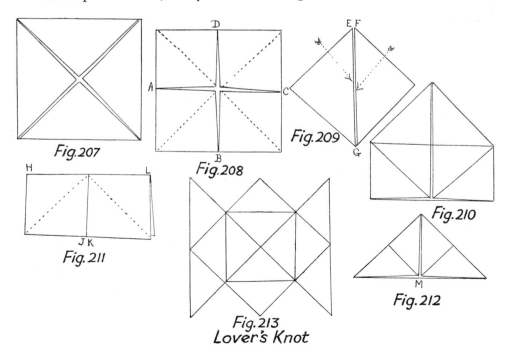

Fig. 207

Fig. 208

Fig. 209

Fig. 210

Fig. 211

Fig. 212

Fig. 213
Lover's Knot

KITE   JAPANESE HELMET   AEROPLANE

LILY   ROSE

BELLOWS   BOOKMARK   CHRISTMAS DECORATION

PLATE II

CHINESE JUNK

1. Fold a square of paper diagonally both ways; undo.
2. Turn paper over and fold straight in half both ways; undo.
3. Turn paper back again, lay flat, and you have Fig. 214.
4. Fold each corner to the centre, and you have Fig. 215.
5. Fold *ABC* to the centre line *HD*; undo.
6. Fold *GFE* to the centre line *HD* (Fig. 217); undo.
7. Fold *AHG* to the centre line *BF*; do not undo.
8. Fold *CDE* to the centre line *BF*, and you have Fig. 218.
9. Fold in half along dotted line *GH* backwards. Lay down like Fig. 219.
10. Fold *J* in Fig. 219 to *G*, and *K* to *H*, letting *L* come up on to *I*, top layer only. The bottom points then go out to the sides (see Fig. 220). Flatten out along dotted lines. Turn over and repeat, and you have Fig. 220.
11. At the spot where arrow points there are two single corners lying on each side of the middle partition. Pull the front one out and you will have Fig. 221.
12. Fold *L* to *O*, *M* to *O*, and *N* to *O*. Turn over and repeat from para. 11, and you have Fig. 222.
13. Fold down along dotted line, one layer only bringing *PS* to *QR*, turn over and repeat, and you have Fig. 223.
14. Open out the centre where arrow points, lay down on the plain surface, with *V* towards you, and you have Fig. 224.

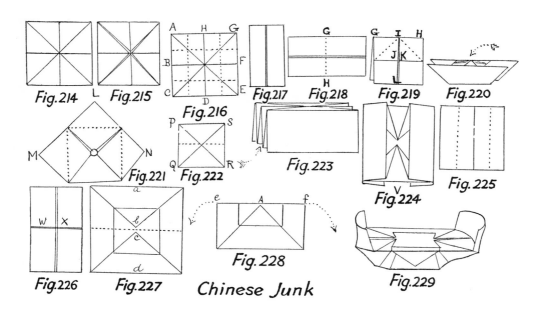

Fig.214   Fig.215   Fig.216   Fig.217   Fig.218   Fig.219   Fig.220

Fig.221   Fig.222   Fig.223   Fig.224   Fig.225

Fig.226   Fig.227   Fig.228   Fig.229

Chinese Junk

15. Fold along dotted lines in Fig. 225 backwards, all layers to the centre, and you have Fig. 226.

16. Draw *W* and *X* apart. Place *b* on *a* and *c* on *d* (Fig. 227).

17. Double this backwards, along dotted line, and you have Fig. 228,

18. Catch centre *A* in your right forefinger and thumb, and gently draw *e* to the left, then catch *A* in your left forefinger and thumb and gently draw *f* to the right.

19. Reverse figure, and pull up the flaps at each end, and you have Fig. 229.

JAPANESE MATCH BOX

This figure must be traced from the Fig. 233; there is no other way of getting it exact. It requires thick and stiff paper. Cut out round outside edge.

1. A fold has to be made along the line *AB* in Fig. 233. This can be done by lifting up the point *O* and inclining it towards the centre, at the same time pinching the paper along *AB*. The folds along the other lines, *BC*, *CD*, *DE*, and *EA*, are made in exactly the same way.

2. A fold has now to be made along the line *IA*. This can be done in the same fashion, by drawing towards each other the points *S* and *O* and pinching the paper along the line *IA*. The folds along *KB*, *LC*, *MD*, and *GE* are made in exactly the same way.

3. When all these lines are well creased, bring the five points *O*, *P*, *Q*, *R*, and *S* together towards the centre. This will cause the sides to fall into place and form the envelope, into which the Bryant and May's Match Booklet can be pasted, but the cardboard cover must be discarded first.

   Fig. 232 shows a novel design which can be painted on each of the five outside surfaces. Fig. 230 shows the upper view of the match box and Fig. 231 the inside.

JAPANESE ASH-TRAY

1. Trace the outline for the Japanese Match Box and draw on all the designs.

2. Fold it up as the matchbox is folded. Undo. Turn over and let it relax, and it will form an ash-tray.

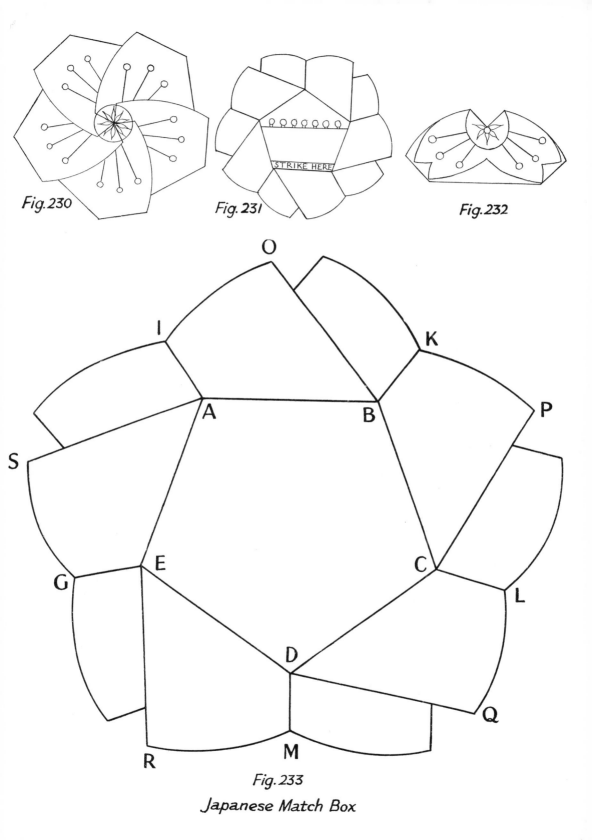

Fig.230

Fig.231

STRIKE HERE

Fig.232

O

I

K

A

B

P

S

E

C

G

L

D

R

M

Q

Fig.233

Japanese Match Box

PAPER BASKET

1. Fold a 6 in. square of paper diagonally once, and you have Fig. 234.
2. Fold along dotted line bringing *A* to *B*, and you have Fig. 235.
3. Fold again along dotted line bringing *C* to *D*, and you have Fig. 236.
4. Fold along dotted line in Fig. 236, bring *E* to *F*, and you have Fig. 237.
5. Make marks along each edge $\frac{1}{2}$ in. apart as shown in Fig. 238.
6. Start cutting every half-inch from the right-hand side, to within $\frac{1}{4}$ in. of the left-hand edge.
7. Turn figure round, and make the left-hand cuts half-way between the cuts already made.
8. Cut along dotted line to make a complete circle. You have sixteen layers folded together now.

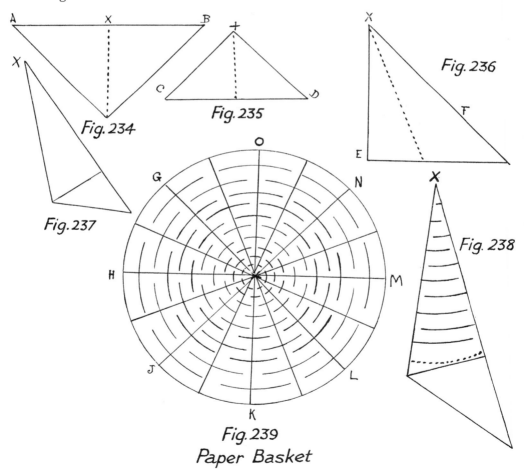

Fig. 234

Fig. 235

Fig. 236

Fig. 237

Fig. 238

Fig. 239
Paper Basket

9. Undo very carefully layer by layer and lay down flat as shown in Fig. 239. Then place a weight in the centre X and gather up loops at G, H, J, K, L, M, N, and O.

10. Tie with a ribbon through the loops.

The X indicates the centre of the paper in each figure.

LIFEBOAT

1. Fold a square of paper diagonally each way; undo.

2. Turn paper over, and fold straight across in half each way, undo, and turn paper again.

3. Fold each corner to the centre, and you have Fig. 240.

4. Turn figure over, and you have Fig. 241.

5. Fold the line AF to the centre line BE.

6. Fold the line CD to the centre line BE. You now have Fig. 242.

7. Turn over, and you have Fig. 243.

8. Fold along dotted lines, top layer only, and bring J to H and K to L, and you have Fig. 244.

9. Turn figure over, and you have Fig. 245.

10. Fold along each dotted line, and you have Fig. 246.

11. Fold along dotted lines in Fig. 246, press heavily, and you have Fig. 247.

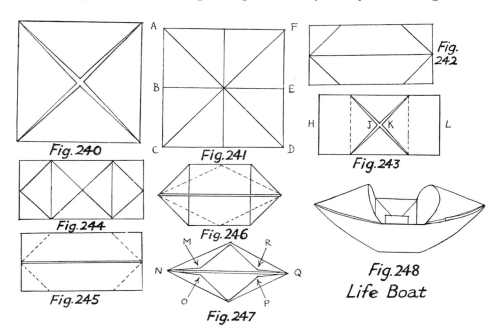

Fig. 240

Fig. 241

Fig. 242

Fig. 243

Fig. 244

Fig. 245

Fig. 246

Fig. 247

Fig. 248
Life Boat

45

12. Grasp three layers of the paper, one side in each hand, where arrows point at *M* and *O*, leaving only *one* thickness, which becomes the bottom of the boat.

13. Turn it very thoroughly inside out. Attend to only one half of the boat at a time, keeping the other end from undoing.

14. Repeat where arrows point at *R* and *P*, at the end marked *Q*. Turn that side inside out also.

15. Adjust the boat nicely inside and pull up the flaps at each end, and you have Fig. 248.

ORNAMENTAL BOX

1. Fold a square of stiff paper diagonally both ways; undo, then fold two corners to the centre, and you have Fig. 249. Paste the points down.

2. Fold backwards along dotted lines and bring the line *AB* along the centre line *AG*. Also fold *AF* along the centre line *AG* on the left. Do the same on the right, folding *ED* along the centre line *HD*, and *CD* along the centre line *HD*. Press these four folds, only as far as the folded corners. Undo.

3. Now pinch up, from behind, the dotted lines in Fig. 251, at *J*, *K*, *L*, and *M*.

Fold along the central square, which lies between dotted corners in Fig. 251, to get the base of the box. Refold as in Para. 2, and keep in fold, while you catch the 2 points *N* and *O*, holding about 1½ in. down, between finger and thumb of your left hand. Press down against the centre of the box; *J* and *L* must fall into position outside *NG* on the left, and *K* and *M* outside *HO* on the right. Paste them at the centre on each side and you have Fig. 250, but with straight points. Curl points round a pencil.

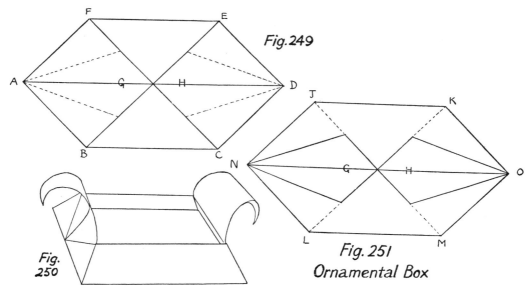

Fig. 249

Fig. 250

Fig. 251
Ornamental Box

JAPANESE ORNAMENTAL BALL

1. Fold a 3″ square of paper diagonally both ways; undo.
2. Turn paper over and fold straight in half both ways; undo.
3. Reverse paper.
4. Fold each corner to the centre, and you have Fig. 252.
5. Fold along dotted lines from *A*, bringing *B* and *H* together on the centre line *AE*. Press well over dotted lines, and undo.
6. Bring *D* and *B* to the centre line *CG*, creasing dotted lines well.
7. Bring *D* and *F* to the centre line *EA*, undo; and bring *F* and *H* to the centre line *GC*, and undo.
8. Draw the four corners together to a point on top.
9. Turn figure upside down, push in the two opposite sides and middle lines, and lay flat like Fig. 254. Crease well.
10. Open out figure as Fig. 253, with the four single corners uppermost. Push up the centre from below, and the figure will relax, into a pretty star-like form as Fig. 255.

The Japanese make six of these, and sew them together at the points till a complete ball is made. Join three squares together at the six top corners, leaving a triangle between the squares; add the other three squares in the same way.

A coloured bead finishes off each corner (see Fig. 256).

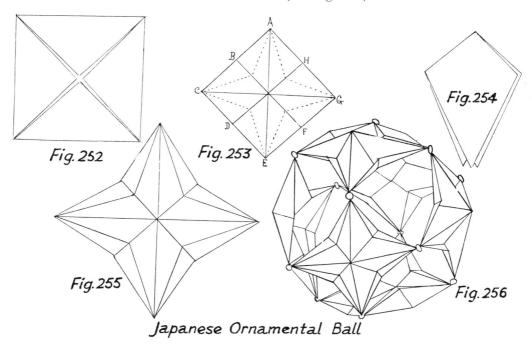

Fig. 252

Fig. 253

Fig. 254

Fig. 255

Fig. 256

Japanese Ornamental Ball

LONG-TOED FROG

1. Fold a square of paper diagonally both ways; undo; do not reverse paper.
2. Fold straight across once, and undo. Reverse paper.
3. Fold straight across the other way, and you have Fig. 257.
4. Raise up *B*, one layer only, and place it on *A*, and paper will fold down into Fig. 258.
5. Turn over and do the same on the other side, and you have Fig. 259.
6. Raise *F* (top layer) to the vertical position over the line *CE*, open out this section, and lay line *CF* exactly over the centre line *CE*. Press flat and you have Fig. 260.
7. Turn figure over and repeat from paragraph 6.
8. Place *I* on *K*.
9. Raise *H* up to the vertical and lay *GH* exactly over the central line *GJ*. Turn figure over, when you have Fig. 261.
10. Place *O* on *Q*.
11. Raise *N* to the vertical and place the line *MN* exactly over the centre line *MP*, and you have Fig. 262.
12. Place *R* on *S*, single layer only. Turn over and do the same on the other side. You now have Fig. 263. Your surface should be, top and bottom, like Fig. 263, four layers each side and the points towards you.

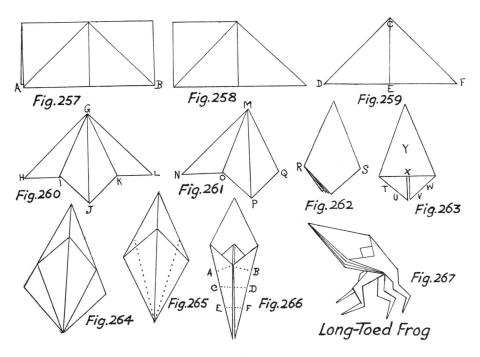

Fig. 257   Fig. 258   Fig. 259
Fig. 260   Fig. 261   Fig. 262   Fig. 263
Fig. 264   Fig. 265   Fig. 266   Fig. 267

Long-Toed Frog

13. Raise the single margins *TU* and *WV* to the centre line and at the same time raise *X* to *Y* on the centre line, and you have Fig. 264.

14. Turn over and do the same on the other side.

15. Then open the centre on both sides in turn and in each case lay flat, and repeat para. 13 (Fig. 263). You now have Fig. 265.

16. Fold (single layer only) along dotted lines to the centre.

17. Turn over and repeat.

18. Open out the centre on both sides, and lay flat. Fold again along the dotted lines as in Fig. 265. Turn over and repeat, and you have Fig. 266.

19. Fold at *A* and *B* up along dotted lines to make the frog's front legs, raising the two top layers.

20. Fold back at *C* and *D* in the opposite directions to make the knees.

21. Fold forward at *E* and *F* to make the ankles.

22. Do the hind legs (lower layers) in the same way, and you have Fig. 267.

Use green paper the same colour on both sides.

THE TABLE

Substantial paper should be used for this model.

1. Fold a square of paper diagonally both ways; undo. Fold straight across both ways and undo.

2. Fold each corner to the centre; undo. This gives you Fig. 268.

3. Fold along each dotted line in Fig. 269, bringing *CBA* to the line *DVH*, also *EFG* to the same line. Do your other two sides, bringing the edges to line *FVB*. Undo, and lay flat, like Fig. 269.

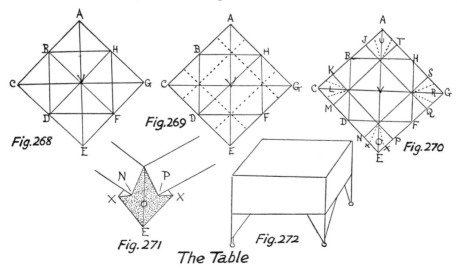

Fig.268

Fig.269

Fig.270

Fig.271

Fig.272

The Table

4. Turn paper over and crease *N* and *P* to *O* (Fig. 270), *K* and *M* to *L*, *J* and *T* to *U*, and *S* and *Q* to *R*. (This will not be found easy but is really simple with a little practice. Fig. 271 illustrates one corner.)

5. Paste down these folds, e.g. *T* to *U* and *J* to *U*, and the other three corners in the same way.

6. Each corner will then make a leg. Fix a match into each corner with glue; the round end will then make a castor, as in Fig. 272.

Paste a strip of paper inside each corner of the table, so that it is out of sight, and holds the match in place.

TABLE-CLOTH

1. Cut a 3 in. square of thin white paper.

2. Fold *B* to *A*, and you have Fig. 274.

3. Fold *C* to *D*, and you have Fig. 275.

4. Fold *E* to *F*, and you have Fig. 276.

5. Fold *H* to *J*, and you have Fig. 277.

6. Turn upside down, and you have Fig. 278.

7. *X* shows the centre of the paper in each figure. Cut out a scalloped edge, and in order to make the design in the table-cloth, cut out the black portion as shown in Fig. 278 or make your own design, being careful never to cut right across from margin to margin.

There are sixteen layers of paper folded together, and when these are undone and laid flat you will have a pretty circular table-cloth, with a symmetrical pattern all over.

A touch of paste here and there will make it lie flat on the table.

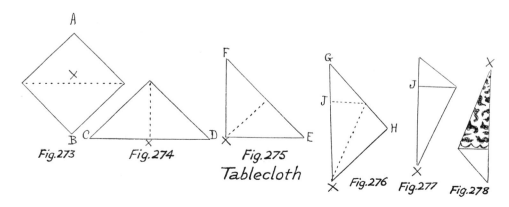

Fig.273   Fig.274   Fig.275
Tablecloth
Fig.276 Fig.277 Fig.278

TABLE-CENTRE

1. Take a 3 in. square of paper. A tinted paper is preferable.
2. Fold diagonally both ways; undo.
3. Turn paper over, and fold straight in half both ways.
4. Undo, lay flat, and you have Fig. 279.
5. Fold corners *A*, *B*, *C*, and *D* to the centre, and you have Fig. 280.
6. Turn paper over, and fold each corner again to the centre. Turn over once more and repeat, then reverse figure, and you have Fig. 281.
7. Roll back points *J*, *K*, *L*, and *M*, and fix the tips with paste so that the sections are not lying flat.
8. Fill centre with small flowers when finished, made from various coloured papers, accordion pleated, and cut small. Directions for these are given below.

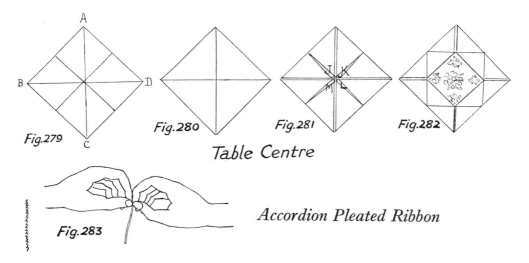

Fig.279 *Fig.280* *Fig.281* *Fig.282*

Table Centre

Fig.283

Accordion Pleated Ribbon

ACCORDION PLEATED PAPER RIBBON

1. Cut a length of thin paper $\frac{1}{16}$ in. wide and about 4 in. long.
2. Hold it at the very end, right-hand side, between your right-hand forefinger and thumb, letting the length of the paper extend over your left thumb.
3. Bring up your left thumb so that the nails of both thumbs catch the paper alternately, with the paper between them. (See Fig. 283.)
4. Click the left thumb nail over the right with the paper between.
5. Then the right thumb nail over the left with the paper between.
6. Do this alternately till the paper is all used up, so that the paper is thrown to the right by the left nail and back to the left by the right nail, keeping the paper exactly at the points of contact between the two thumb nails.

With a little practice you can keep up the clicking noise faster than the ticking of a clock. Now decorate the umbrella handle (page 34) with the pleated paper, and fix with paste.

Also use it in different colours, and cut in short lengths, to fill the table-centre in imitation of flowers; a touch of paste in the centre piece will hold it all in position.

TABLE NAPKIN

This requires a piece of paper 1½ in. square.

1. Fold diagonally both ways; undo. Turn paper over.
2. Fold straight across in half each way; undo (see Fig. 284).
3. Place *W* and *Y* on *X* as indicated in Fig. 285.
4. Press *V* down on to *X*, spreading out the points *C* and *A*, and you will have Fig. 286.
5. Fold *CD* and *AD* along the dotted lines shown in Fig. 286, and you will have Fig. 287.
6. Turn paper over and do the same with the other two points *EG*, and you will have Fig. 288.
7. Fold up as shown by dotted line in Fig. 288 on both sides and the napkin is made.

Four of these are required to furnish the table.

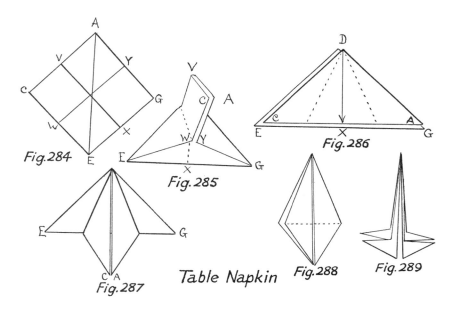

Fig.284

Fig.285

Fig.286

Fig.287

Table Napkin

Fig.288

Fig.289

GUESTS

The sixteen guests are made from one piece of paper 8 in. square.

1. Fold *A* to *B* and you have Fig. 291.

2. Fold *C* to *E* to get the centre line. Undo.

3. Fold the line *CF* down along the centre *FD*, also *FE* along *FD*, and you have Fig. 292. Fold along dotted lines and you have Fig. 293.

4. Fold *K* backwards to *J*, and you have Fig. 294. Lay flat as shown in Fig. 295. Cut along the dotted line *LM*.

5. You now have sixteen layers folded together and each one makes a guest. Draw a guest on the top layer only, as shown in Fig. 296, and cut through all the layers with sharp scissors, and you have Fig. 297. N.B. Do not cut through the ends of the arms, however, as the guests are held together at these points. (See Fig. 298.)

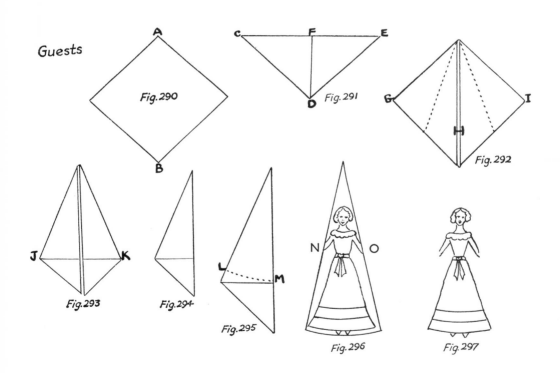

Guests

Fig. 290

Fig. 291

Fig. 292

Fig. 293

Fig. 294

Fig. 295

Fig. 296

Fig. 297

A full-sized diagram shows the sixteen figures flattened out—Fig. 298.

Paint in dresses, faces, and hair with water-colours and place them round the table (for table, see Fig. 272).

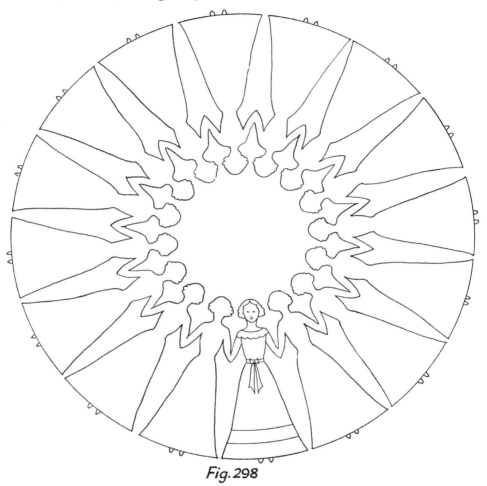

Fig. 298

INFLATED FROG

This requires a 7 in. square of thin, white, tough paper which you must paint with water-colours to imitate the colouring of a frog.

1. Fold the paper straight across in half both ways, undoing after each fold. Turn paper over, then fold diagonally, both ways, undoing after each fold, and you have Fig. 299.

2. Paint all the shaded portion dark green, and when quite dry cover it with darker spots, black or dark brown. Paint the white portion yellow, and when dry cover with vermilion spots. This makes the frog's breast. Let it dry thoroughly.

3. Turn paper over and lay it on the table with white side up. Fold along dotted lines in Fig. 300, thus bringing E to F and G to F. Do not undo. Turn figure over and fold along dotted lines again in Fig. 301, bringing H to I and J to I. Do not undo. Turn figure over, and you have Fig. 302. Undo. The remaining three corners must be folded in the same way. Fig. 303 shows the creases in one finished corner. When all are done, undo and lay flat, with white side up.

4. Fold each corner to the centre. Turn figure over and you have Fig. 304. Mark in pencil the points O, P, Q, and R, 2 in. from each corner as in Fig. 304.

5. Fold each corner along dotted line bringing K to O, L to P, M to Q, and N to R, and you have Fig. 305.

6. Now fold along the dotted line in Fig. 305 between T and X, taking Z backwards to V. Press the fold heavily with your thumb-nail. Undo. Now fold along the line between U and Y, bringing W backwards to S. Press and undo.

7. Next fold along between V and Z, bringing X backwards to T. Press and undo, and lastly fold between W and S, taking U backwards to Y. Press and undo. Fold XW to ST and press the centre line straight across, undo, then fold UV to ZY and again press the line; undo.

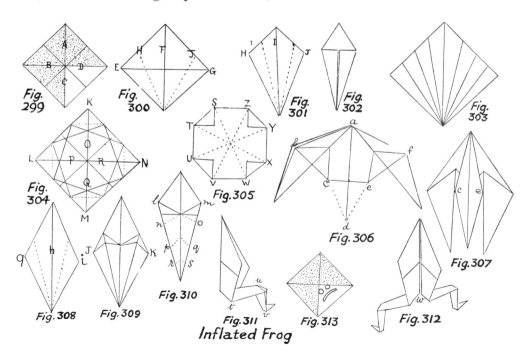

Fig. 299
Fig. 300
Fig. 301
Fig. 302
Fig. 303
Fig. 304
Fig. 305
Fig. 306
Fig. 307
Fig. 308
Fig. 309
Fig. 310
Fig. 311
Fig. 313
Fig. 312

Inflated Frog

55

8. Now the figure, instead of being flat, must be elongated like Fig. 306. This can be done by drawing down the four corners from below, and pushing up the centre *a*. The four corners must come down to form the frog's feet. Do this without disarranging the four triangles on the top. It is easier to do only two at a time, as in Fig. 306.

9. Push in the centre line *ad* between *c* and *e* (Fig. 306), and bring *c* and *e* together. This forms the first leg of the frog. Push in the centre lines of the other three corresponding surfaces to form the other three legs. Figure can now be collapsed and laid flat as Fig. 308.

   Examine the figure now, and you should have four plain surfaces and four with triangles in the centre. Lay figure flat with a plain surface top and bottom, four layers each side, and four points towards you.

10. Raise one layer on the left, and fold *g* to *h* along dotted line in Fig. 308, then fold *i* to *h* and you have Fig. 309. Turn right over and do the same on the other side. Open out the centre on both sides and lay flat. Fold again as you did in Fig. 308. When all the four surfaces have been folded like Fig. 308, you will have Fig. 310.

11. Now you must fold up the legs, one at a time. To make a foreleg, bend up leg along dotted lines from *n* and *o*, and at the same time bring *l* and *m* together. Bend down at *p* and *q* to make the knee, reversing the centre line. Bend up at *r* and *s* to make the ankle, again reversing the centre line as shown in Fig. 311. Make the second foreleg to match the first. The hind legs should be made slanting as shown in Fig. 312.

   Inflate by blowing in aperture at *w*. Add a mouth and eyes at the top of the yellow breast as in Fig. 313. This may be done before the folding is begun.

FIRST FOUNDATION

1. Fold a square of paper diagonally both ways (colour outside); undo. Turn paper over and fold straight across in half both ways; undo. Reverse paper again, and you have Fig. 314.

2. Fold each corner to the centre, and you have Fig. 315. Do *not* undo.

3. Fold along each of the dotted lines in Fig. 315, undoing after each fold.

4. Push up the centre from below *E*, and make the corners all come together, so that a smaller square is formed. Place figure on the table with the centre *G* towards you, and the four points away from you at *F*, and you have Fig. 316.

5. Open out where arrows point at *A* and *B*, so that *F* comes over on to *G*.

6. Turn over and repeat, and you have Fig. 317.

7. Fold *I* up to *H* top layer only; use a forefinger or pointed pencil to arrange the two triangles which form at each end when paper is flattened, as shown in Fig. 318 (apexes *K* and *L*).

SNAKE	COCKROACH		CUTTLEFISH		POPLAR TREE
HOODED FROG		BUTTERFLY		BULL FROG
FLYING BIRD		FISH	INFLATED FROG

PLATE III

8. Turn over and do the same on the other side.
9. Place *JK* single layer on *ML*.
10. Turn over and do the same on the other side, and you have Fig. 319.

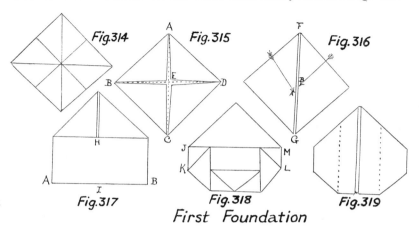

Fig.314   Fig.315   Fig.316

Fig.317   Fig.318   Fig.319

First Foundation

BOX ON FOUR FEET

Start at Fig. 319 on First Foundation, page 56.

1. Fold *R* to *S* and *T* to *S*; undo. Fold the short dotted lines up (one layer only); the other dotted lines when folded will keep them in place. Fold *R* and *T* to the central line again.
2. Turn over and repeat on the other side. The four points make the feet.
3. Fold *U* down to *V* one layer only, turn over and repeat on the other side. Then fold along dotted line *YZ* (one layer) as shown in Fig. 321. Turn over and repeat.
4. Draw these handles apart and at the same time push up *W*, and you have Fig. 322.

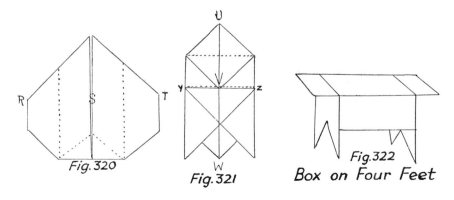

Fig. 320   Fig. 321   Fig. 322

Box on Four Feet

COW

Start with Fig. 319 on First Foundation (page 56)—see Fig. 323.

1. Fold *A* to *B* and *C* to *B*. Turn over and do the same on the other side, and you have Fig. 324.

2. Fold *D* to *E* (top layer); turn over and do the same on the other side, and you have Fig. 325.

3. Cut along dotted line on the right, remove *J* entirely, and the part remaining between *F* and *G* makes the cow's tail; bend this down behind.

4. Cut along left-hand dotted lines between *H* and *G* (all layers), to within $\frac{1}{4}$ in. of the centre line. The strips thus formed will make the horns. With a sharp pen-knife make a slit, about $\frac{1}{4}$ in., at the smaller dotted line marked *I*.

5. Unfold head, cut horns free at points, lay model flat, and you have Fig. 326. The strips cut at *H* in Fig. 325, the cow's horns, must be pushed upward (see *K* and *L* in Fig. 326), then bent and pulled through the slits made at *I* in Fig. 325. In doing this bend down the triangle to make the face—see Fig. 327.

6. Next make the ears, by folding down the corners *M* and *N* in Fig. 327 along the dotted line *OP*, and also along *QR*, then fold backwards along the smaller dotted lines, near *M* and *N* as shown in Fig. 328.

7. Now push up the centre from below *S* in Fig. 325; this will make a square box. Cut out the feet back and front, as shown in Fig. 328. Draw eyes and nostrils. Bend the horns round to make them resemble the twists in a cow's horns.

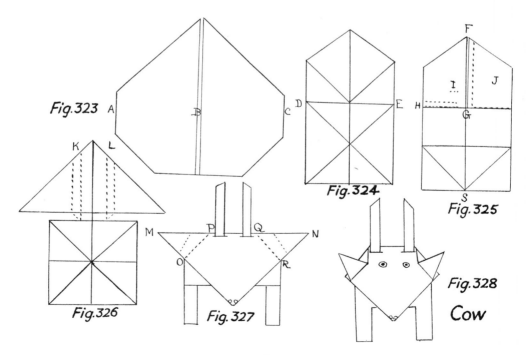

Fig. 323   Fig. 324   Fig. 325   Fig. 326   Fig. 327   Fig. 328   Cow

A leather punch makes good eyes, a large size for the whites, and a smaller size made of black paper, for the pupils. Paste them together.

If the cow be made of white paper, put black spots on it, to resemble a Friesland.

LEMUR

Start at Fig. 319 in First Foundation—see Fig. 329.

1. Fold along dotted lines, bringing *A* and *C* to the centre *B*. Turn over and repeat, and you have Fig. 330.

2. Place *D* on *E* (one layer), turn over and repeat, and you have Fig. 331.

3. Cut along dotted lines in Fig. 331. The right-hand side makes the head and ears, and the left makes the tail. The portion marked *K* must be cut away. Fold *F* to *G* and lay flat.

4. Push up *O* and open out the box, and get it out of the way while you cut out the legs. Cut at *L* and *M* along dotted lines in Fig. 332. Turn over and repeat to make the hind legs.

5. Unfold the ears, and bring the head down as in Fig. 332. Add eyes and nostrils, and you have Fig. 333.

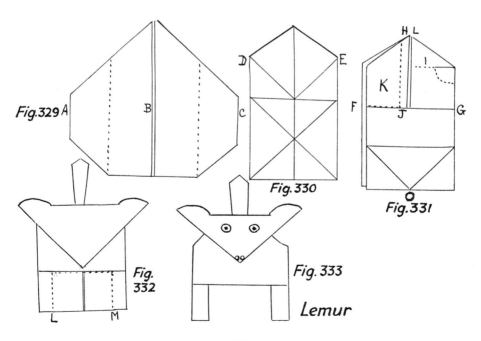

THE MAN

This is made with two 5 in. squares of paper and made in two portions which join at the waist.

1. Take the first square, fold diagonally both ways, and undo.
2. Fold each corner to the centre, and you have Fig. 334.
3. Turn paper over, and fold each corner to the centre again, and you have Fig. 335.
4. Turn paper over again, and fold each corner to the centre a third time, reverse paper again, and you have Fig. 336.
5. Open slot between *E* and *F*, and place *E* on *F*, and you have Fig. 337. This becomes the man's waist, as shown by dotted lines in Fig. 339 between *J* and *K*.
6. Now partly undo figure, by raising up *B* in Fig. 337 and carrying it beyond *A* as far as it will go, and by raising up *C* and carrying it beyond *D* as far as it will go (keep in place the waist fold—see bottom dotted lines in Fig. 339). Look at the back and see that it looks like Fig. 338.
7. Turn to the front again, bend back the triangular fold at the top so that it lies on the other side, turn paper over to this side and press the top well.
8. Fold along the dotted line in Fig. 339, bringing *GH* to *JK*.
9. Pick up the four corners *G*, *H*, *K*, and *J* and push them simultaneously inward to the centre *X* in Fig. 338 (to achieve this, folds must fall into place along

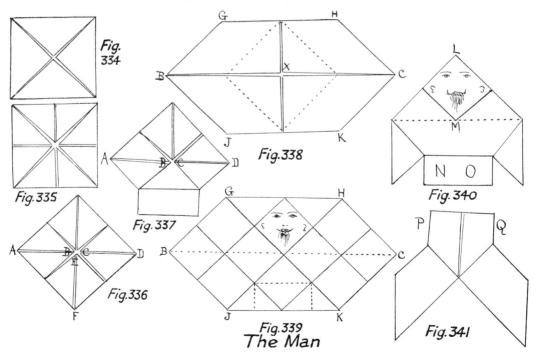

Fig. 334 · Fig. 335 · Fig. 336 · Fig. 337 · Fig. 338 · Fig. 339 · Fig. 340 · Fig. 341

The Man

the dotted lines in Fig. 338). As you do this, you must let the points *B* and *C* stand up.

10. Turn down points *B* and *C* to make the man's arms, turn over, and you have Fig. 340.
11. Draw the man's face.
12. For the legs, take the second square of paper and fold again as above down to Fig. 340.
13. Open slot between *M* and *L* and place *M* on *L*.
14. Fold up *NO* to *LM* along the dotted line, and you have Fig. 341.
15. *PQ* must be pushed up inside the waist of the man's body at *NO* (Fig. 340) and fixed with paste.

THE HORSE

Starts at Fig. 319 of First Foundation. Fold A to B and C to B. Turn over and repeat on the other side, and you have Fig. 343.

1. Fold *QR* to *TS*, one layer only, turn over and repeat, and you have Fig. 344.
2. Fold along dotted line, bringing down point *A* between the folds on the left side to make the head as in Fig. 345.
3. Bring down point *B* in the same way, between the two folds on the right, to make the tail.
4. Cut out along dotted lines *YW*, *WX*, and *XZ* to make the legs.
5. Cut the tail as shown in Fig. 346.
6. Add eyes.

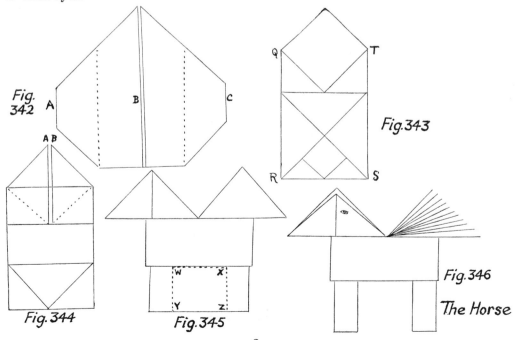

Fig. 342

Fig. 343

Fig. 344

Fig. 345

Fig. 346

The Horse

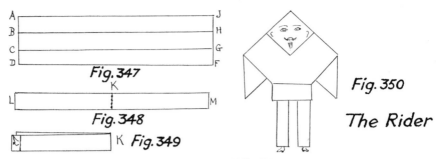

Fig. 347

Fig. 348

K Fig. 349

Fig. 350

The Rider

THE RIDER

The rider is so small, that you should practise making the man on page 60, *before attempting to make the small rider.*

To fit a horse made from a 6 in square of paper use a 3 in. square. Then make the rider's body in the same way as the man's body (p. 60).

To Make the Legs

1. Cut paper ¾ in. wide and 3 in. long.
2. Fold *DF* up to *BH*, then fold *AJ* down over that to *CG*, and you have Fig. 348.
3. Paste these together along the whole length.
4. Fold *M* to *L* along dotted line *K*, and you have Fig. 349.
5. Cut out feet together on the double, then cut at *K*, making two legs, which must be pasted inside the waist belt, as shown in Fig. 350.
6. Paint the boots black.

The man looks well in red paper.

Put him astride the horse (p. 61).

SECOND FOUNDATION

1. Fold a square of paper diagonally both ways; undo.
2. Fold across straight in half once only; undo.

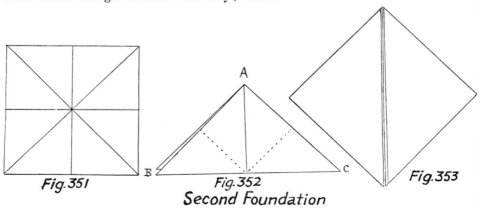

Fig. 351

Fig. 352
Second Foundation

Fig. 353

3. Turn paper over and make the other straight fold. Lay flat and you have Fig. 351.

4. Push up the centre of the paper and the inverted fold will readily fall into its place, and you will have Fig. 352.

5. Fold along dotted lines, placing *B* and *C* on *A* (top layers only).

6. Turn figure over and do the same on the other side, and you have Fig. 353.

THE KETTLE

This starts at Fig. 353 of the Second Foundation.

Place figure down with the four single ends away from you (X in Fig. 354).

1. Fold along dotted lines in Fig. 354, top layer only, bringing *A* to *B* and *C* to *B*.

2. Turn figure over and repeat, and you have Fig. 355.

3. Undo to Fig. 354, both back and front.

4. Carry point *D* down to the left as shown in Fig. 356. Lay flat and press.

5. Raise *G* to *E* and you have Fig. 358 (see picture of this fold, Fig. 357).

6. Fold back *D* along dotted line *CB* to *E*, as shown in Fig. 358.

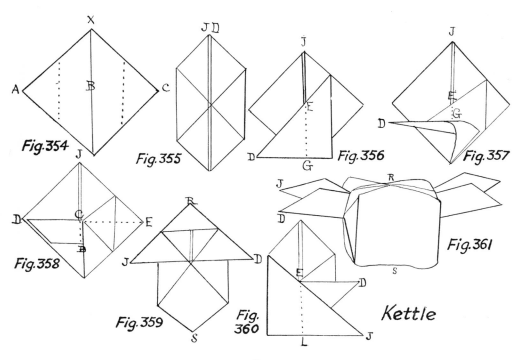

63

7. Carry point *J* down to the right side as shown in Fig. 360; fold *L* on *E* as before, and fold point *J* over to the left opposite to *D* (Fig. 359).

8. Turn figure over and repeat from para. 4.

9. Fold handle *J* to *D*, Fig. 359, turn over and repeat, and you have Fig. 361, which gives the view of the kettle when inflated.

To inflate blow into the opening at *R* and at the same time push up point *S*. Half fill with water, and boil over a candle flame, holding it by the two handles each side. Blow out the candle with the bellows, which come next to the kettle in this book.

BELLOWS

Start at Fig. 353 of Second Foundation.

1. Lay figure down with the four single points towards you (see *X*, Fig. 362).

2. Fold top layer along dotted lines in Fig. 362, *A* and *C* to *B*; undo.

3. Turn over and do the other side; undo.

4. Fold top layer along dotted lines in Fig. 363, *A* and *C* to *E*; undo.

5. Turn over and do the other side; undo, and you have Fig. 364.

6. Pinch the points *M* and *N* together, and *O* and *P* together, two top layers, and push them to meet in the centre as in Fig. 365.

7. Repeat on the other side, and you get Fig. 366, which is a side view.

8. Hold *NM* together in one hand, and *OP* in the other, draw them apart, and push them together sharply.

These bellows will easily blow out a candle.

The blast will be improved by cutting off a small portion with scissors, where the air escapes.

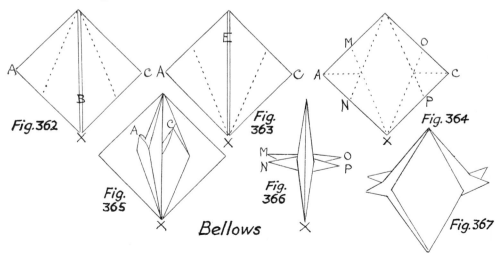

Fig.362 Fig. 363 Fig. 364 Fig. 365 Fig. 366 Bellows Fig.367

WATER BOMB

Start with Fig. 353 on Second Foundation, page 62, as shown here in Fig. 368.

1. Fold *A* and *C* to *B* (one layer), and you have Fig. 369.
2. Turn over and do the same on the other side, and you have Fig. 370.
3. Fold the two single points *E* and *F* down to the centre, along dotted lines. Do not undo. Turn over and repeat on the other side.
4. Fold along dotted lines in Fig. 371. Undo. Turn over and repeat on the other side.
5. Push *M* into the slot between *H* and *O*, Fig. 371, and push *N* into the slot between *J* and *O*. They must disappear entirely. Turn over and repeat on the other side, and you have Fig. 372. Turn figure upside down and inflate by blowing into the point marked *Q*, at the same time pressing *P* up gently, and you have Fig. 373.

   Filled with water, this becomes a missile for mischievous boys.

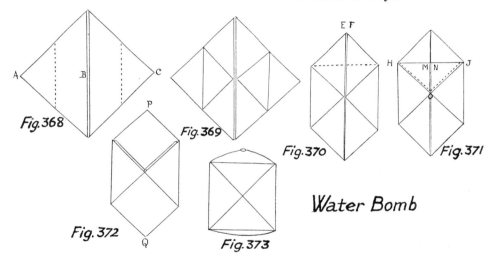

Fig. 368

Fig. 369

Fig. 370

Fig. 371

Fig. 372

Fig. 373

Water Bomb

CHINESE LANTERN

Start at Fig. 353 on Second Foundation—see Fig. 374.

1. Fold along dotted lines in Fig. 374, top layer only, bringing *A* to *B* and *C* to *B*.
2. Turn over and do the same on the other side, and you have Fig. 375.
3. Fold along dotted lines in Fig. 375, one layer only, bringing *E* to *O* and *F* to *O*, and you have Fig. 376.
4. Turn over and do the same on the other side.
5. Fold along dotted lines in Fig. 376; undo.
6. Push the point *M* into the slot between *H* and *O*; also push *N* into the slot between *K* and *O*. They must lie flat between the layers.

7. Turn figure over and repeat on the other side.

8. Inflate the lantern by blowing into the hole at *J*, then turn figure upside-down and you have Fig. 377.

9. Fig. 378 shows the shape the wire handle must be.

   Fix one end of handle at *P* and *Q* with an ornamental picture scrap to hold it in place. Turn figure over and do the same on the other side, and you have Fig. 379.

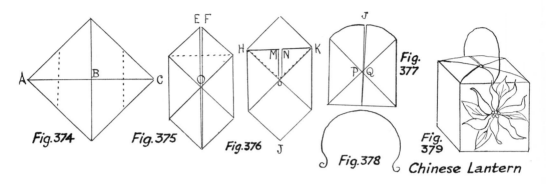

Fig. 374   Fig. 375   Fig. 376   Fig. 377   Fig. 378   Fig. 379   *Chinese Lantern*

THIRD FOUNDATION

1. Fold a square of paper diagonally both ways (colour outside); undo.

2. Fold straight across in half once only; undo.

3. Turn paper over and make the other straight fold, undo, and you have Fig. 380.

4. Push up the centre of the paper and the inverted fold will readily fall into place (see Fig. 381), and you have Fig. 382.

5. Raise up *L* to make it stand vertically (see Fig. 383).

6. Open out this section a little, and press *LM* down the centre, immediately on to the line *MK*, and you have Fig. 384.

7. Fold *O* on to *P* along dotted line in Fig. 384, raise up *N*, and do the same as you did to *L*, starting from para. 6.

8. Turn paper over and treat the other two points in the same way, and you have Fig. 385.

9. Arrange so that you have a plain surface top and bottom and four folds on each side (Fig. 385). Fig. 386 shows transition stage for next diagram.

10. Place *U* (single layer) on *S*, hold the point down tightly with your left forefinger whilst you fold each of the outside single margins in to the centre line. A pointed pencil will help at the angles which form at points *C* in Fig. 387.

11. Turn over and repeat, and you have Fig. 387.

12. Open out the centre of each side and lay flat like Fig. 385, and repeat from para. 10.

13. Raise up *B*, top layer, Fig. 387, and carry it down beyond *C*, as far as it will go; repeat on the other side, and you have Fig. 388.

14. Place *D* on *E*, raising two layers; turn over, and repeat also raising two layers, and you have Fig. 389.

15. Bring *F*, one layer only, down to *G*; turn over and repeat, and you have Fig. 390.

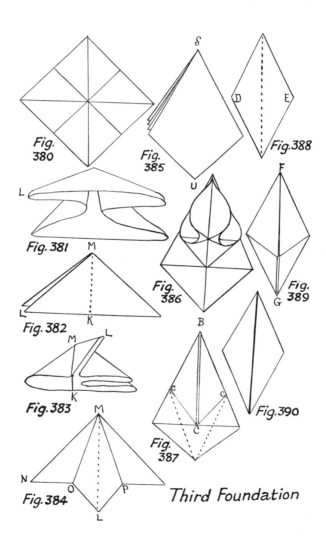

Fig. 380

Fig. 385

Fig. 388

Fig. 381

Fig. 386

Fig. 389

Fig. 382

Fig. 383

Fig. 390

Fig. 387

Fig. 384

Third Foundation

KANGAROO

Start at Fig. 390 of the Third Foundation. In this figure you have four plain surfaces and four with triangles.

1. The triangles must be reversed as in Fig. 391 by placing *A* on *B*; repeat with the other three triangles, and lay figure down with a plain surface top and bottom, four layers on each side, and the four points towards you, and you have Fig. 392.

2. Fold along dotted lines top layer only, putting *C* on *D*, and *E* on *D*, and you have Fig. 393.

3. Turn over and repeat. Find the centre of each side where arrow points; lay flat and repeat the fold in para. 2, and you have Fig. 394.

4. Place *H* on *I* (Fig. 394), turn over and repeat, and you have Fig. 395.

5. Insert finger in Fig. 395 where arrows point at *J* and *K*, raising one ply only, and bend up the front legs *L* and *M* as shown in Fig. 399.

6. Figs. 396, 397 and 398 show how to fold the legs. Bend up at dotted lines in Fig. 396, inverting the central fold as shown in Fig. 397. Fig. 398 gives the side view.

7. Fold up these two front legs, as shown in Fig. 399, between the two top layers *O* and *P* on the left and the corresponding two top layers on the right.

8. Bend along the dotted lines in Fig. 399, and the two short front legs are completed as shown in Fig. 401.

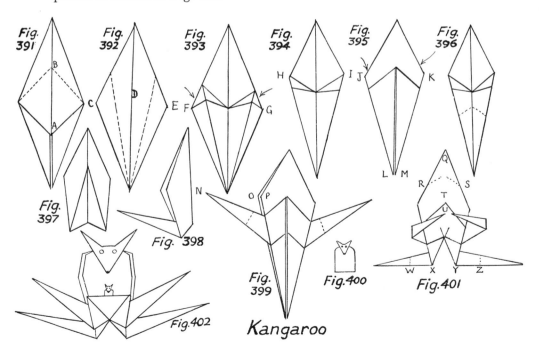

Fig. 391 Fig. 392 Fig. 393 Fig. 394 Fig. 395 Fig. 396

Fig. 397 Fig. 398 Fig. 399 Fig. 400 Fig. 401 Fig. 402

Kangaroo

9. Fold up the hind legs in the same way at *X* and *Y* but at the lower angle, again inverting the centre line, then fold along dotted lines at *W* and *Z* to complete.

10. Fold *U* to *V*, Fig. 401, to make the pouch.

11. Cut with scissors along dotted lines at *R* and *S*, through all the layers; leave the centre uncut.

12. Place *Q* on *T*, when the two points *R* and *S* will stand up and become the kangaroo's ears. Add eyes. Cut out Fig. 400, and paste into pouch, as shown in Fig. 402.

COCKROACH

Start at Fig. 390 of Third Foundation—Fig. 403.

1. Place *A* on *B* (one layer), and you have Fig. 404; turn over and repeat.

2. Take *E* up to *C*, and similarly reverse the other three triangles which are between the plain surfaces of the figure.

3. Lay figure down flat with a plain surface top and bottom four layers each side and the four points next to you, and you have Fig. 405.

4. Fold along dotted lines bringing *G* and *H* to the centre line. Turn and do the same on the other side.

5. Open out the centre of each side and lay flat like Fig. 405.

6. On both these plain surfaces fold along dotted lines again (as para. 4), and you have Fig. 406.

7. Now fold up between *I* and *J*, to make a leg, inverting the centre line, as shown in Fig. 407.

8. Then turn down between *K* and *L* to make the knee, again inverting the centre line, in the opposite direction.

9. Turn up between *M* and *N* to make the ankle as shown in Fig. 408.

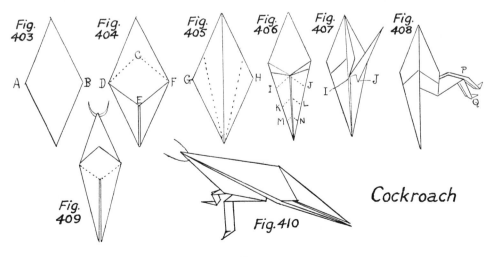

Cockroach

69

10. Do the same to the next layer on the left and make the folds exactly at the same angles, so that the two legs match exactly.

11. Undo the two folds shown by dotted lines in Fig. 405, to make the back and wings of the cockroach.

12. Turn down the triangle as shown in Fig. 409 by dotted lines.

13. Cut a strip of paper pointed at each end, to imitate the antennae of the insect, and insert it as shown in Fig. 409, and you have Fig. 410.

CUTTLEFISH

Start at Fig. 390 of Third Foundation—Fig. 411.

1. Fold *A* to *B* and reverse the triangle as shown in Fig. 412, by placing *C* on *D*. Do the same to the triangles between all the other surfaces.

2. Lay figure down with a plain surface at top and bottom, and four layers each side, and the four points towards you.

3. Fold *E* and *F* (Fig. 413) along the dotted lines to *G* and you have Fig. 414.

4. Turn over and do the same on the other side.

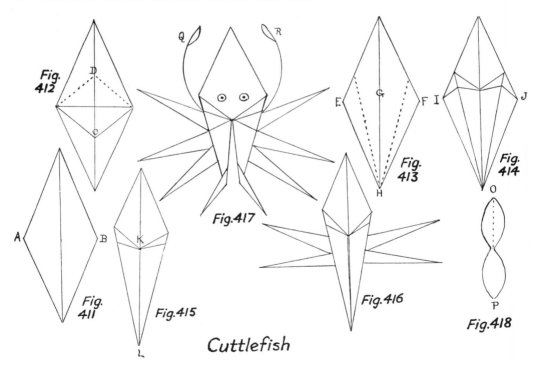

Cuttlefish

5. Open out the centre on each side and do the same to the other two surfaces, and you have Fig. 415.

6. Cut each point from *L* to *K* in the centre, single layer only. Bend right-hand front point backwards up under first fold. At a lower angle bend up the second point, and place it behind the second fold. Do this to both the right and left sides. Fig. 416 shows the angles for the first four points.

7. Fold the other points at various angles as shown in Fig. 417. Turn the model the other way up, as shown in Plate III, and add antennae and eyes.

To Make the Antennae

1. Fold in half two pieces of paper, each $1\frac{1}{4}$ in. $\times$ $\frac{1}{2}$ in.

2. Open out separately, and cut out each one to shape shown in Fig. 418.

3. Cut a narrow rubber band in the centre, place one end along dotted line in Fig. 418, enclose it by pasting *P* on *O*. Repeat at the other end. Insert the centre of rubber band behind the first folds and fix with paste. They should hang down on each side of the face. Draw the eyes.

BULL FROG

Start at Fig. 390 of the Third Foundation—Fig. 419.

1. Between each plain surface you will find one with a triangle. These triangles must all be reversed and your figure should be laid down like Fig. 419, with four layers each side and four points next to you.

2. Fold the line *AC* along the dotted line to the centre, also fold *BD* along the dotted line to the centre. Turn over and do the same on the other side. Open out the centre on both sides, and lay flat and fold again as you did Fig. 419, and you will have Fig. 420.

3. Fold *G* up as far as it will go, between the top two layers, reversing the centre line at the dotted line *E*. Also fold *H* up as far as it will go, between the top

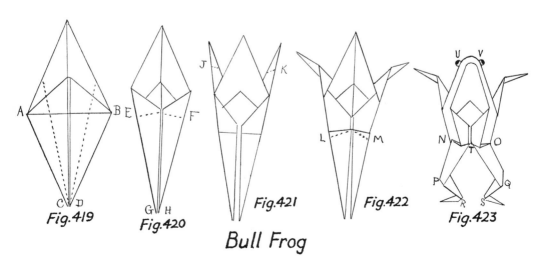

Fig. 419   Fig. 420   Fig. 421   Fig. 422   Fig. 423

Bull Frog

two layers, reversing the centre line at the dotted line *F*. This makes the two front legs as shown in Fig. 421.

4. Bend at *J* and *K*, reversing the centre line, to make the toes as shown in Fig. 422.

5. Pinch up small pleats at *L* and *M* on both layers to alter the direction of the hind legs (see *N* and *O* in Fig. 423).

6. Reverse the centre line at *P* and *Q*, raising one layer only to make the knees, and bend in the opposite directions at *R* and *S* to form the ankles, also inverting the centre line there.

7. Inflate the body by blowing into the small aperture at *T*.

8. To add the bulging eyes, squeeze thick chinese white out of a tube, on the two spots *U* and *V*, and when they solidify paint the pupils in the centre with ink.

HOODED FROG

Start at Fig. 390 of Third Foundation—Fig. 424.

Use green paper for this model.

1. Fold *A* to *C*, to find the triangle. There are four plain surfaces and four have triangles. All the triangles must be reversed as shown in Fig. 425 by placing *F* on *E*.

2. Lay figure down with a plain surface top and bottom, four layers on each side, and the four points towards you, and you have Fig. 426.

3. Fold along dotted lines top layer only, placing *G* on *H* and *J* on *H*, and you have Fig. 427. Turn over and do the same on the other side. Place *K* on *L*, turn over and do the same on the other side, and fold the two surfaces top and bottom, as you did Fig. 426. You will now have Fig. 428.

4. Now fold the legs. Raise *S* up and fold along dotted lines *S* and *T*, inverting the centre line. The side view is shown at *U* in Fig. 429. Bend down at *OP*,

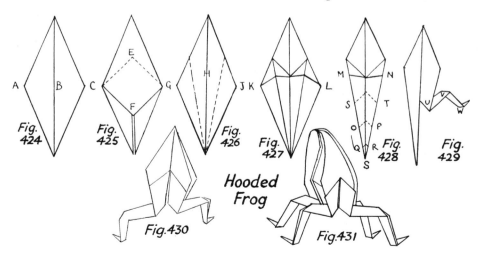

Fig. 424

Fig. 425

Fig. 426

Fig. 427

Fig. 428

Fig. 429

Hooded Frog

Fig. 430

Fig. 431

inverting the centre line again to make the knee, and fold up at *QR* to make the ankle. Fig. 429 shows these three folds at *U*, *V*, and *W*.

5. Bring *M* and *N* together and press all the folds heavily.

6. Fold the adjoining point at *S* at exactly the same angles, so that the two front legs match exactly. Measure it against the completed leg. The hind legs are folded at a lower angle as shown in Fig. 430. Make the two hind legs in the same way to match exactly, and you have Fig. 430.

7. Now, to make the hood, leave the two centre layers between the forelegs, catch the next layer on each side, with forefinger and thumbs. Pull them apart and gently forward, and you have Fig. 431.

FOURTH FOUNDATION

1. Fold paper straight across both ways; undo.

2. Fold diagonally one way; undo.

3. Turn paper over and make the last diagonal line in the opposite direction; undo. Remember this inverted fold, which makes it easy to collapse the figure when you come to Fig. 439.

4. Turn paper over to original side.

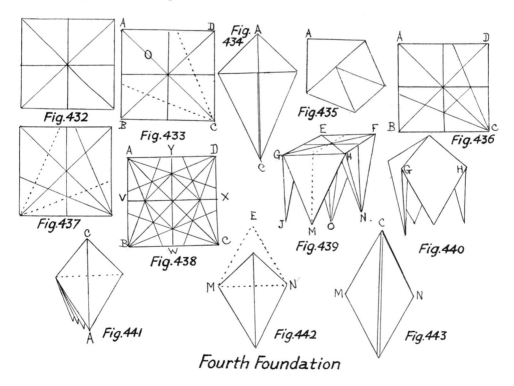

Fourth Foundation

73

5. Fold along dotted lines in Fig. 433, bringing *B* to *O* and *D* to *O*, and you have Fig. 434.

6. Fold *C* to *O*, and you have Fig. 435. Undo paper and lay flat, and compare the lines with those in Fig. 436.

7. Fold each corner, as you have done this first one. Fig. 437 shows you how to go on with your second corner. Fig. 438 shows the folds you must have when all the corners are done.

8. Press in the middle of each side margin, marked *V*, *W*, *X*, and *Y* in Fig. 438 and the square in the centre seen in Fig. 438 becomes the square marked *EFHG* in Fig. 439. Turn figure up the other way, with the points downward, so that *A*, *B*, *C*, and *D* in Fig. 438 are the points *J*, *M*, *N*, and *O* in Fig. 439. (Be sure that *V*, *W*, *X*, and *Y* remain pressed in.)

9. Push up the centre, holding the four corners *E*, *F*, *G*, and *H* (Fig. 439) with the thumbs and second fingers so that the inverted crease *MO* lies under the first fingers.

10. Press the inverted crease gently inwards with the first fingers, at the same time pressing *G* to *E* and *H* to *F*, and the model will collapse, and form Fig. 441. Fig. 440 shows the start of this fold.

11. Fold *A* in Fig. 441 (top layer) upwards along dotted line, and place it on *E*, Fig. 442. Turn figure over and repeat, and you have Fig. 443.

KITE

This starts at No. 441 in Fourth Foundation—Fig. 444.

With a needle and cotton attach the tail, sewing through the four points at *U* in Fig. 444. Tie folded paper at equal distances and fix a bunch at the end to complete the tail. Ornament with cut paper at the top and at corners *V* and *W*.

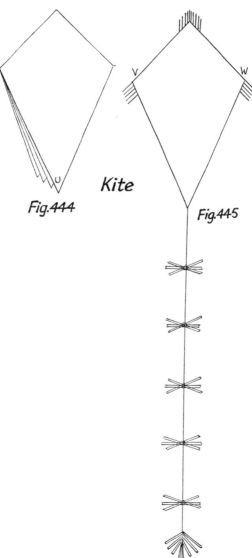

Kite

Fig.444

Fig.445

THE FISH (SHARK)

This starts at Fig. 443 of Fourth Foundation—Fig. 446—with the divided points towards you.

1. Fold M and N to B and you then have Fig. 447.
2. Turn paper over and repeat, and you have Fig. 448.
3. Fold the top layer at N over M.
4. Turn over and repeat, and you have Fig. 449.
5. Cut out the fins and paste them between the two layers of paper in their correct positions.
6. At the tail end bend each half separately, turning inwards along dotted lines shown in Figs. 449 and 450; this will form the tail.
7. Paint in eyes and gills.

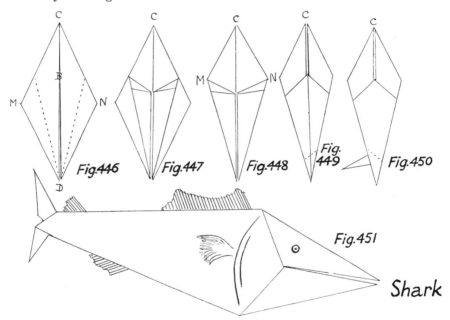

Fig.446 Fig.447 Fig.448 Fig. 449 Fig.450

Fig.451

Shark

THE FLYING BIRD

This begins at Fig. 443 of Fourth Foundation.

1. Bring M to N (top layer) in Fig. 443, turn figure over and do the same on the other side, and you have Fig. 452.
2. Fold E to B (top layer). Turn figure over and do the same on the other side, and you have Fig. 453.
3. Now make the bird's beak, by bending down point A to the left, inverting the central fold, as shown in Fig. 454. Fold down the wing B along dotted line in Fig. 454. Turn model over and do the same to wing D on the other side.

4. By holding the point on the breast at *S* (all layers) between the finger and thumb of the left hand, and moving the tail *C* backwards and forwards, the wings will be made to flap.

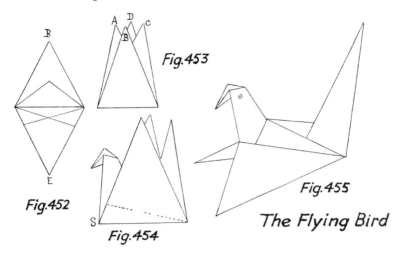

Fig.452

Fig.453

Fig.454

Fig.455

The Flying Bird

PENGUIN

Start at Fig. 443 of the Fourth Foundation, but place the divided end away from you, so that the separated points are at the top—see D in Fig. 456. Use black paper.

1. Fold *A* to *B* and *C* to *B*, single layers. Now you have Fig. 457.

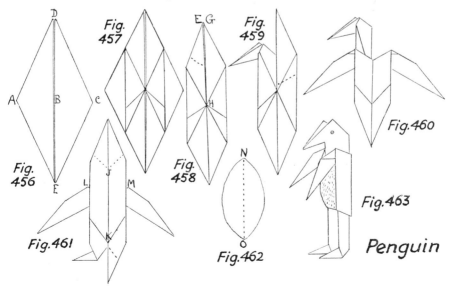

Fig. 457

Fig. 459

Fig. 460

Fig. 456

Fig. 458

Fig. 461

Fig. 462

Fig. 463

Penguin

2. Turn paper over and repeat, and you have Fig. 458.
3. Fold *E* down along the dotted line to make the head, reversing the middle fold as shown in Fig. 459. Then cut the remaining upright piece down the middle, from *G* to *H* in Fig. 458, to make the flippers. Now you have Fig. 459.
4. Fold each flipper along dotted line in Fig. 459. The flippers are then folded round the body, one on each side, to protrude below the head (this means that the uncut lower part of each of these two sections must also be folded round). Fig. 460 shows the flipper on the left in position.
5. Fold up the feet along the dotted lines in Fig. 461, in the same way as you did the head, reversing the middle fold.
6. Cut out the breast, from white paper, as shown in Fig. 462. Open out the body and paste the breast inside the figure from *J* to *K* in Fig. 461, placing *N* at *J* and *O* at *K*. Fold *M* on to *L*, and you have Fig. 463. Paint in the eyes.

OPEN BOX

1. Fold a square of paper straight across in half both ways; undo.
2. Fold across diagonally both ways; undo; lay flat.
3. Fold each corner to the centre, and you have Fig. 464.
4. Fold along the dotted lines, bringing *AHG* to the middle line *BF*, also *CDE* to *BF*. Undo.
5. Fold *ABC* to the middle line *HD*, also *GFE* to *HD*. Undo.
6. Draw *M* and *Q* apart, and lay flat as in Fig. 465.
7. Fold the line *KL* to the middle line *MQ*, also the line *NOP* to *MQ*, and you have Fig. 466. Fold along the line *RZ* and also along *SA*, and undo.

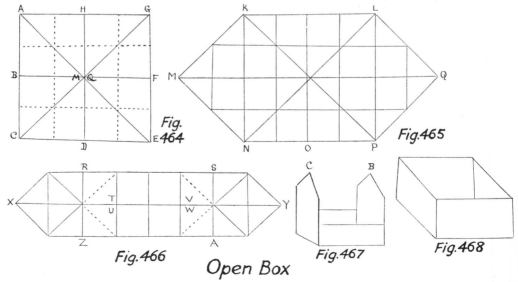

Fig. 464

Fig. 465

Fig. 466

Fig. 467

Fig. 468

Open Box

8. Raise *T* up to *R* along dotted line, also *U* to *Z* along dotted line; this will cause *X* to stand vertically, like *C* in Fig. 467.

9. Fold *V* to *S* and *W* to *A*, and *Y* will stand erect, like *B* in Fig. 467, and you have Fig. 467.

10. *B* and *C* must now be folded down so that the tips meet in the centre of the box, and securely enclose the side folds. You then have Fig. 468.

ROSE

1. Fold a square of paper diagonally both ways; undo.
2. Fold each corner to the centre, and you have Fig. 469.
3. Turn figure over and fold the four corners to the centre again.
4. Turn figure over; again fold the corners to the centre, press the folds firmly.
5. Undo all folds up to Fig. 469.
6. Place *A*, *B*, *C*, and *D* (Fig. 470) on the centre *O*. This will cause the four corners *E*, *F*, *G*, and *H* to stand up as in Fig. 471.
7. Press *E* down upon the centre. Do this to *F*, *G*, and *H* and you will have Fig. 472.
8. Curl back petals, *JKLM*, round a very thin pencil.
9. Gently pull together points *N*, *O*, *P*, and *Q* on the underneath layer.

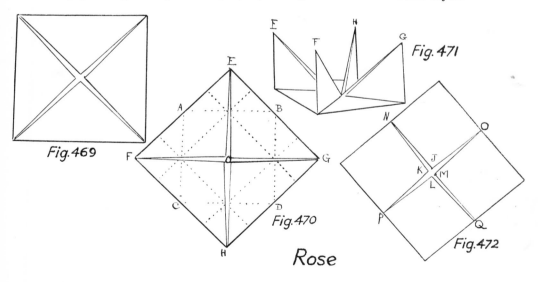

Fig. 469

Fig. 470

Fig. 471

Fig. 472

Rose